The Ten Commandments

The Ten Commandments

"The Law of Liberty"

By
Taylor G. Bunch

ORION *PUBLISHING*

P. O. Box 449
Ukiah, CA 95482
800-471-4284

Copyright © 2002
Orion Publishing   All Rights Reserved

Cover and Layout Design by
Greg Solie - Altamont Graphics

ISBN# 0-9659327-8-8 $12.95
Printed in Canada

CONTENTS

FOREWORD

The importance of a series of studies on the decalogue is emphasized by the fact that it deals with the summary of all truth and therefore embraces "the whole duty of man."

The law of God demands a careful and prayerful consideration by every free moral agent living under its jurisdiction and subject to its penalties, and this includes the whole human race. Obedience to it is the evidence of love and loyalty, and has in all ages been the distinguishing mark that has separated the worshipers of the true God from the devotees of all false deities and counterfeit religious concepts.

The ten commandments constitute the only part of divine revelation given directly by God Himself without the assistance of a human instrument. The decalogue was spoken by the voice of God under circumstances that sent its message rolling down through the millenniums of time to our day, and on into the endless cycles of eternity. Its precepts were chiseled by the finger of God in tables of lasting granite to indicate their value and perpetuity.

Through the gospel the same eternal law that sums up all human duties and relationships is rewritten by the Holy Spirit on the fleshy tables of the heart, so that the Word is again made flesh and God's will is done on earth as it is in heaven.

The new covenant experience magnifies and enforces the righteous demands of the law in the daily life, so that one can say with Christ, *"I delight to do Thy will, O My God: yea, Thy law is within My heart."*

This book was written for and is dedicated to the purpose of emphasizing the spiritual nature and lessons of the decalogue, with the hope and prayer that the reader may know from experience the imputed and imparted righteousness of Christ that makes it indeed the law of liberty.

Taylor G. Bunch

THE LAW OF GOD

I
Thou shalt have no other gods before Me.

II
Thou shalt not make unto thee any graven image, or any likeness of anything that is in heaven above, or that is in the earth beneath, or that is in the water under the earth: thou shalt not bow down thyself to them, nor serve them: for I the Lord thy God am a jealous God, visiting the iniquity of the fathers upon the children unto the third and fourth generation of them that hate Me; and showing mercy unto thousands of them that love Me, and keep My commandments.

III
Thou shalt not take the name of the Lord thy God in vain; for the Lord will not hold him guiltless that taketh His name in vain.

IV
Remember the Sabbath day, to keep it holy. Six days shalt thou labor, and do all thy work: but the seventh day is the Sabbath of the Lord thy God: in it thou shalt not do any work, thou, nor thy son, nor thy daughter, thy manservant, nor thy maidservant, nor thy cattle, nor thy stranger that is within thy gates: for in six days the Lord made heaven and earth, the sea, and all that in them is, and rested the seventh day: wherefore the Lord blessed the Sabbath day, and hallowed it.

V
Honor thy father and thy mother: that thy days may be long upon the land which the Lord thy God giveth thee.

VI
Thou shalt not kill.

VII
Thou shalt not commit adultery.

VIII
Thou shalt not steal.

IX
Thou shalt not bear false witness against thy neighbor.

X
Thou shalt not covet thy neighbor's house, thou shalt not covet thy neighbor's wife, nor his manservant, nor his maidservant, nor his ox, nor his ass, nor anything that is thy neighbor's.

THE DIVINE RULE OF LIFE

1

"God *spake all these words, saying, I am the Lord thy God, which have brought thee out of the land of Egypt, out of the house of bondage."* **Exodus 20:1, 2.** Although this statement does not constitute an integral part of the law of the ten commandments, its importance is emphasized by the fact that it is the preface or prologue to the great fundamental rule of life for all men in all ages. It indicates, first of all, that the ten precepts about to be proclaimed are applicable to all mankind. The reason is then given as to why they should be received and obeyed by the Israelites, to whom they were directly proclaimed.

The Speaker and Lawgiver was the One who had so mightily and miraculously delivered them from the power of Pharaoh and the bondage of Egypt. He had abundantly demonstrated His unlimited power and sovereign authority over the greatest nation on earth and His superiority over the gods of the Egyptians. The ten plagues followed by the mighty deliverance had proved that *"the Lord is a great God, and a great King above all gods"; "the Lord is great, and greatly to be praised: He is to be feared above all gods. For all the gods of the nations are idols: but the Lord made the heavens."* **Psalms 95:3; 96: 4, 5.**

In the giving of the decalogue, the Creator, the God *"who made the heavens,"* was speaking. He was also their Redeemer who had delivered them from the bondage of Egypt, which was typical of the far greater deliverance from the slavery of sin and its author, Satan. The same law applies with equal force to all who are delivered by the gospel from the darkness and bondage of spiritual Egypt down through all ages and dispensations. This prologue to the law is beautifully paraphrased by **Isaac Watts:**

"I am the Lord; 'tis I proclaim
That glorious and that fearful name,
Thy God and King; 'twas I that broke
Thy bondage, and the Egyptian yoke;
Mine is the right to speak My will;
And thine the duty to fulfill."

UNIVERSAL SOVEREIGNTY

"I am the Lord thy God" is a declaration of divine sovereignty, an assertion of supreme and everlasting dominion and rulership. This declaration or its equivalent is the preamble to every divine promise, warning, precept, and proclamation recorded in Holy Writ. Because He is the Lord of all, He has a right to command and to require obedience of all His creatures. *"Thy God"* indicates that obedience is an individual responsibility. It cannot be done by proxy. The moral law summons each person individually to the judgment bar of God. The obedience of one can never atone for the disobedience of another.

The Ruler of the universe prefaced the giving of His law with a series of mighty miracles to effect the emancipation of His people from a cruel slavery that was both physical and spiritual, and to bring punishment upon their oppressors. After making them free, He gave them *"the perfect law of liberty"* (James 1:25; 2:12) that they might remain free. *"I will walk at liberty: for I seek Thy precepts"* (Psalms 119:45), declared the psalmist, and a well-known maxim of the modern world is, "Obedience to law is liberty." Herbert Hoover declared that "liberty lives by law." Law is absolutely necessary to freedom and civilization.

A noted Jewish scholar declared that the decalogue was proclaimed at Mount Sinai rather than in Palestine to indicate that it was given, not for the Jews alone, but for all peoples and races in all ages. For the giving of the law the Lord chose a time which precluded any thought of its having a human origin. Such a code of morals could not possibly have come out of Egyptian civilization, saturated with gross idolatry, nor from a race of Hebrew slaves who had mingled with the Egyptians.

The decalogue bears the stamp of divine origin and authorship. The impressive and spectacular manner in which the law was given was for the purpose of emphasizing this great fact. (See **Exodus 19:1-19.**) The voice of God was loud and distinct, not alone for the benefit of the hosts of Israel on the plain below the seven-thousand-foot granite peak from which He spoke, but also for the benefit of all mankind as it would go rolling down through the ages.

THE LAWGIVER

The spelling of the word "LORD" in capital letters identifies the lawgiver as Jehovah, as it is translated in the American Revised Version. Jehovah is a combination of three Hebrew words indicating the eternal, ever-living, self-existent God. "I am the Eternal," is the James Moffatt translation, and "I am your ever-living God," is the rendering by Ferrar Fenton. He is the great "I AM" who was, and is, and is to come. He is *"the high and lofty one that inhabiteth eternity."* Isaiah 57:15. "LORD" and "Jehovah" indicate the Redeemer as well as the Creator; the One with the power to make and remake, create and recreate. Christ is therefore identified as the lawgiver, as He is declared to be in **Isaiah 33:22** and **James 4:12.**

That Christ is the Creator is evident from many texts. (See **John 1:14; Ephesians 3:9; Colossians 1:13-19; Hebrews 1:1-3; Revelation 3:14.**) Only the Creator can redeem or re-create. Both require the same omnipotent power. Likewise, only the Lawgiver can redeem from the curse, penalty, or condemnation of the law.

A well-known writer said:
"Christ was not only the leader of the Hebrews in the wilderness,-the Angel in whom was the name of Jehovah, and who, veiled in the cloudy pillar, went before the host,-but it was He who gave the law to Israel. Amid the awful glory of Sinai, Christ declared in the hearing of all the people the ten precepts of His Father's law. It was He who gave to Moses the law engraved upon the tables of stone."
–E. G. WHITE, *Patriarchs and Prophets*, p. 366.

That Christ was the divine leader of ancient Israel during their journey from Egypt to Canaan is clearly stated in **1 Corinthians 10:1-4.**

13

The law is a revelation of the very nature of the Lawgiver, a transcript of His character. The same expressions are used throughout the Scriptures in describing God and His law, showing that they are inseparable in character. Both are declared to be perfect, holy, righteous, good, just, eternal, and unchangeable. The decalogue is therefore the expression of the eternal and unchangeable principles of right inherent in the very nature or character of God. Since the principles of right can never change, the moral law that proclaims them can never change or become obsolete.

The holiness, justice, perfection, and righteousness that belong to the law, belong also to the Lawgiver. The decalogue is organic, fundamental, and constitutional. It is the foundation of the throne and government of God. Being an expression of the nature and character of God, the law must be as perpetual as God Himself, for the nature of God never changes.

LAW OF PRINCIPLES

To *"fear God, and keep His commandments"* is declared to be *"the whole duty of man"* in **Ecclesiastes 12:13**, or *"the duty of all men"* in the margin of the Revised Version. This is because the law constitutes a summary of all right principles. The first table with its four commandments reveals in brief man's whole duty to His Maker, and the second table with its six precepts sets forth man's whole duty to his fellow men. Jesus declared that on these two tables, defining our love to God and man, *"hang all the law and the prophets."* (**Matthew 22:36-40.**) The entire Bible is therefore an unabridged edition of the decalogue, and the law is a summary of the Scriptures. The psalmist said, *"Thy commandment is exceeding broad."* **Psalms 119: 96.**

This law of God's nature was implanted in the nature of man at his creation when he was *"made in the image of God."* When Adam was created, the first table of the law began to operate and regulate his duty toward his Creator. When Eve was created, another relationship, which must be defined by law, sprang into existence between creatures, and the second table automatically began to apply. Both tables must continue in force as long as the Creator and any of His creatures exist. For this reason the law was in existence before man was created, to regulate the duties of angels and the inhabitants of other worlds, and it must continue through all eternity.

The requirements of love and the regulations of duty are as perpetual as the necessity for them. The Lord wrote the principles of His moral law in the mind and upon the fleshy tables of man's heart at creation, and before sin came into the world they operated as naturally and spontaneously as the laws of nature do in the physical world. It was as natural for man to do the will of God as for the birds to fly, the trees to grow, and the flowers to blossom. Although sin has changed man's nature, the law of God has not been entirely erased. This is evident from **Romans 2:14-16**: *"When the Gentiles, which have not the law, do by nature the things contained in the law, these, having not the law, are a law unto themselves: which show the work of the law written in their hearts, their conscience also bearing witness, and their thoughts the meanwhile accusing or excusing one another."*

This scripture declares that even the heathen have in their hearts and consciences a sense of right and wrong which if followed will bring salvation. Those whose characters have been changed by the power of God have His image restored in them and under the new covenant experience the law is again written in the mind and upon the fleshy tables of the heart, so that they *"do by nature the things contained in the law."* It again becomes natural to obey God and unnatural to disobey.

Righteousness is first of all right being, which is far more fundamental and important than right doing. Right doing is the fruit of right being. We must be good before we can do good. If we are right we will do right. We can then say with Christ, *"I delight to do Thy will, O My God: yea, Thy law is within My heart."* **Psalms 40:8**. The apostle declared, *"This is the love of God, that we keep His commandments: and His commandments are not grievous."* 1 John 5:3. One writer has beautifully set forth the results of love-obedience:

> *"All true obedience comes from the heart. It was heart work with Christ. And if we consent, He will so identify Himself with our thoughts and aims, so blend our hearts and minds into conformity to His will, that when obeying Him we shall be but carrying out our own impulses."*
> –E. G. WHITE, *The Desire of Ages*, p. 668.

This is genuine Christianity. A religion that is considered a sacrifice or burden is spurious. The gospel is good news and glad tidings. It brings joy and peace, hope and contentment.

A REIGN OF LAW

The entire physical universe is under the dominion of law. Everywhere unseen and intangible forces are operating in the control and direction of all things.

There is nothing anywhere that is not governed by law unless it be sinful and rebellious man. The casting aside of law would soon bring chaos and ruin to all things, animate and inanimate, organic and inorganic. All law is the expression of the will and a manifestation of the character of the Lawgiver. Natural law is the operation of principles which the Creator implanted in all His creatures, according to the nature and purpose of each. God is the author of all these laws, and from Him they derive the impelling power that makes them operate.

The moral law was in the same way divinely implanted in the nature of man at creation. At Sinai this law was put in written form. Paul declared that *"it was added because of transgression."* Galatians 3:19. It was not the institution of a new law but the proclaiming of the original law of man's being in a new and permanent form because of the increase of sin or lawlessness. All laws carry a penalty for the transgressors, whether they be natural or moral. The man who puts his hand in the fire or steps off a precipice must suffer the penalty of natural law. The same is true when we transgress the laws of our being in eating and drinking. Moral law must also be obeyed or the penalties endured. There is no escape, even though the day of reckoning is often delayed. The penalty is always sure in the end. The wages of sin must be fully paid by someone-if not by the transgressor, by a Substitute, who meets the demands of the law in his stead. Justice must be satisfied.

A PERFECT LAW

Since none of God's laws are arbitrary enactments, but are rather enunciations of eternal principles of right which grow out of the very nature of that which is governed, they are therefore as

16

perfect and eternal as the character of the Creator and Lawgiver. The psalmist said of the law, *"I have seen an end of all perfection."* **Psalms 119:96.** He also said, *"The law of the Lord is perfect, converting the soul."* **Psalms 19:7.** This latter statement doubtless applies to the laws of nature as well as to the moral law. The psalmist had just been describing the movements of the heavenly bodies in obedience to natural law. Since the moral law is based on the nature of God, it is of necessity perfect and eternal. God never changes, and therefore His laws can never change.

It is estimated that man has enacted more than thirty-two million laws in an effort to regulate human conduct, but he has never yet caught up with the decalogue. The laws of man must be constantly changed, amended, or abrogated to keep legislation up to date. Thirty thousand new laws are enacted each year in the Federal and State legislatures of the United States. In one bill Congress repealed more than one thousand old and out-of-date laws, and the State of New Jersey eliminated twelve hundred obsolete laws at one time. The decalogue is both brief and comprehensive, and was given in its written form thirty-five hundred years ago; yet it has never needed to be altered or even amended in the least particular. It is just as up to date and applicable to the needs of mankind today as when it came from the mouth and the hand of the Eternal. This alone is enough to prove its divine origin.

AN ETERNAL LAW

The psalmist said of the Lord, *"The works of His hand are verity and judgment; all His commandments are sure. They stand fast forever and ever, and are done in truth and uprightness."* **Psalms 111: 7, 8.** In the **119th Psalm** of twenty-two sections of eight verses each, the word "commandments" is used twenty-two times. Read it through carefully and notice how he exalts and even revels in the commandments of God. The statement of the wise man applies with special force to the perpetuity of the law of God: *"I know that whatsoever God doeth, it shall be forever: nothing can be put to it, nor anything taken from it: and God doeth it, that men should fear before Him."* **Ecclesiastes 3:14.**

An infidel once read the books of Moses in order to prove them untrue. After reading the ten commandments, he made this confession:

17

"I have been looking into the nature of that law. I have been trying to see whether I could add anything to it, or take anything from it, so as to make it better. Sir, I cannot! It is perfect!... Where did Moses obtain that law, which surpasses the wisdom and philosophy of the most enlightened ages? He lived at a period comparatively barbarous; but he has given a law in which the learning and sagacity of all subsequent time can detect no flaw. Where did he obtain it? He could not have soared so far above his age as to have devised it himself. I am satisfied where he obtained it. It came down from heaven. It has convinced me of the truth of the religion of the Bible."
–D. L. MOODY, *Weighed and Wanting*, pp. 13, 14.

Moody himself said of the law:

"Men may cavil as much as they like about other parts of the Bible, but I have never met an honest man that found fault with the ten commandments. Infidels may mock the Lawgiver and reject Him who has delivered us from the curse of the law, but they can't help admitting that the commandments are right." "The commandments of God given to Moses in the mount at Horeb are as binding today as ever they have been since the time when they were proclaimed in the hearing of the people."
–**Id.**, pp. 11, 15.

Let us notice some other striking testimonies in regard to the decalogue:

"The ten commandments persist because they are moral axioms as fundamental in social order as are the axioms of mathematics in the physical sciences.... The ten commandments are practical, adequate, and binding today. They are all we need for modern morality. All our ills and evils are ultimately the price the modern man pays for denying and defying them."
–J. B. ROUNDS, *The Ten Commandments for Today*, p. 5.

"But these commandments, as I have already reminded you, hold a conspicuous position in that prolonged revelation of Himself, of His character, His will, and His relations to mankind, which God made to the Jewish people. They can,

18

therefore, never become obsolete. The changing circumstances of the human race cannot destroy the significance and worth of any institutions or facts which reveal the life of God."

–R. W. DALE, *The Ten Commandments*, p. 5.

"Next to the revelation of divine love in Palestine, the declaration of divine will in Egypt is the greatest event which the world has seen, the most powerful moral force in history . . . No moral system ever humanly formulated before or since . . . can approach, much less equal, or excel, these ten words of God. For all time, human duty is condensed and declared with an authority which, in its divinity, can be neither surpassed nor superseded.

"God and man, religion and morality, the sum of divine and human relationships, what God requires of man, what man owes to God, are all included. However much the revelation of God's will may be amplified, however far the righteousness of man's walk may be advanced, the range of the moral law will never be surpassed."

–JOHN BURR,
Studies on the Ten Commandments, pp. 1, 11.

"The highest civilization the world has yet reached has not gone beyond, has not even attained to the carrying out of these principles. No reason has been discovered for setting aside a single command as unworthy of God or man. Neither is there any prospect that man will ever become conscious, during this earthly stage of his existence, of a principle of his being which is not covered by the law of God, nor of a 'fitness of things' not provided for, nor of a way of securing happiness other than obedience to it."

–FERDINAND S. SCHENCK,
The Ten Commandments, p. 8.

Of this "perfect law of liberty" we can truly say that "higher has the human thought not yet reached."

Let us notice one more testimony written by a well-known modern historian:

"In reviewing the Mosaic legislation, we notice both those

19

ordinances which are based on immutable truth for the rule of all nations to the end of time, and those prescribed for the peculiar situation and exigencies of the Jews as a theocratic state, isolated from other nations.

"The moral code of Moses, by far the most important and universally accepted, rests on the fundamental principles of theology and morality. How lofty, how impressive, how solemn this code! How it appeals at once to the consciousness of all minds in every age and nation, producing convictions that no sophistry can weaken, binding the conscience with irresistible and terrific bonds-those immortal ten commandments, engraven on the two tables of stone, and preserved in the innermost sanctuary of the Jews, yet reappearing in all their literature, accepted and reaffirmed by Christ, entering into the religious system of every nation that has received them, and forming the cardinal principles of all theological belief!...

"All Christian nations have accepted these ten commandments, even Mohammedan nations, as appealing to the universal conscience-not a mere Jewish code, but a primary law, susceptible of boundless obligation, never to be abrogated; a direct injunction of the Almighty to the end of time.... They seem to be designed not merely for Jews, but for Gentiles also, since there is no escape from their obligation. They may seem severe in some of their applications, but never unjust; and as long as the world endures, the relations between man and man are to be settled on lofty moral grounds."

–JOHN LORD,
Beacon Lights of History, Vol. II, pp. 107-110.

PURPOSE OF THE LAW

That the law plays an important part in conversion is evident from the statement of the psalmist, *"The law of the Lord is perfect, converting the soul."* The law is the weapon, or instrument, in the hands of the Holy Spirit by which men are convicted of sin. Sin is divinely declared to be *"the transgression of the law."* 1 John 3:4. Paul declared that *"where there is no law, there is no transgression,"* and that *"sin is not imputed when there is no law."* Romans 4:15; 5:13. The purpose of the law, therefore, is to define sin and convince sinners of its exceeding sinfulness. The apostle says: *"Now we know*

20

that what things soever the law saith, it saith to them who are under the law: that every mouth may be stopped, and all the world may become guilty before God. Therefore by the deeds of the law there shall no flesh be justified in His sight: for by the law is the knowledge of sin." Romans 3:19, 20.

The law and the gospel work hand in hand in the redemption of sinful man. The law cannot take away sin. That was the purpose of the coming of the Saviour, who *"was manifested to take away our sins."* 1 John 3:5. Jesus did not come to take away the law, but rather the transgressions of the law. All the law can do is to convince a guilty sinner that he is under the penalty of eternal death. Pardon and cleansing must come through Christ and the gospel. Before a sick man will apply the remedy of the physician, he must be convinced that he is sick. Before a man can realize his need of a Saviour, he must be made to realize that he is a sinner, and that is the purpose of the law.

For this reason the law and the gospel cannot be enemies. Salvation and righteousness by law are an impossibility. If it were possible the tragedy of Calvary would have been unnecessary. Paul's epistles to the Romans and the Galatians are commentaries on the relationship between the law and the gospel, showing that both are necessary in the plan of redemption. This relationship is beautifully set forth in **Romans 7:7-14; 8:1-14.**

Charles Wesley gave the law its proper place in his preaching. He said that he first gathered his congregations at the foot of the mount of the law to hear the divine standard of righteousness and be placed under the conviction of sin and the condemnation of eternal death. He brought them to the place of hopelessness expressed by the apostle Paul in the seventh chapter of Romans, and in the following poem:

"My sins appeared but small before,
Till terribly I saw
How perfect, holy, just and pure,
Was Thine eternal law.
Then felt my soul the heavy load,
My sins revived again;
I had provoked a dreadful God,
And all my hopes were slain."

21

In this hopeless and undone condition Wesley led his congregation to the mount of Calvary and revealed to them the way of escape. He gave them the remedy for the terrible disease of sin. He showed them the "fountain opened to the house of David... for sin and uncleanness," in which a man can plunge and be cleansed from all his guilty stains. Under deep conviction of sin his hearers were ready to hear the good news of salvation through faith in the atoning blood of Immanuel, the God-man.

This method of preaching the gospel is still orthodox. It is not out of date and never will be. A balanced presentation of the law and the gospel will lighten the earth with the glory of God when *"the everlasting gospel"* is proclaimed to the ends of the earth under the latter rain of pentecostal power, when the Lord *"will finish the work, and cut it short in righteousness: because a short work will the Lord make upon the earth."* Romans 9:28.

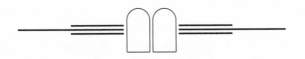

THE TRUE OBJECT OF WORSHIP

2

That there is a close relation between obedience and spiritual vision is evident from the statement, *"Where there is no vision, the people perish: but he that keepeth the law, happy is he."* Proverbs 29:18. The same is indicated by the prayer of the psalmist, *"Open Thou mine eyes, that I may behold wondrous things out of Thy law."* Psalms 119:18.

Spiritual vision illuminates the law, and obedience to the law increases spiritual vision until its revelations are wonderful. Viewing the decalogue under the magnifying glass of spiritual vision convinces us that it is so *"exceeding broad"* that it embraces *"the whole duty of man,"* and that on the two tables which set forth man's duties to his Creator and to his fellow men *"hang all the law and the prophets."*

The law is indeed a summary of divine revelation. It is the Bible in miniature. Jesus came into the world to *"magnify the law,"* and to *"make it honorable,"* and it is through His teachings that our eyes are open to its spiritual import. The gospel always magnifies rather than nullifies the law. *"Do we then make void the law through faith?"* asked the apostle Paul. He then answered, *"God forbid: yea, we establish the law."* Romans 3: 31.

DIVISIONS OF THE LAW

The decalogue was divinely divided into two parts, as indicated by the two tables of stone on which it was written by the finger of

23

God. The purpose of this division is clear. The first table, with its four commandments, regulates man's duty to his Creator. The person who loves God with supreme affection will observe these precepts. The second table, with its six commandments, regulates man's duties toward his fellow men. If we love our neighbors as we love ourselves, we will naturally observe these commandments.

The law is also divided into ten separate precepts. (**Deuteronomy 4:13**.) It is for this reason that the law is called "the decalogue." *Deca* indicates ten, and *logos* means words. It is the ten words or laws. There has been a difference of opinion as to the identity of some of the ten. The Jews generally count the preface as the first commandment and unite the commands against idolatry and image worship. The Roman Catholics and the Lutherans make one command out of what is usually known as the first two and divide the command against covetousness, following the custom of Augustine. Protestants in general use the division adopted by the Greek and Reformed churches. This division was accepted by Josephus, Philo, Origen, the Protestant Reformers, and most of the modern Bible students.

THE FIRST COMMANDMENT

"I am the Lord thy God.... Thou shalt have no other gods before Me," or *"beside Me"* (Revised Version), is the first of the ten commandments. In this precept the Lord proclaims Himself the true God. He is therefore the one true object of worship. Pagan Rome would gladly have accepted Jesus Christ as one of their many gods, but they were unwilling to acknowledge Him as the Son of the one and only true Deity. It is even difficult for many who claim to worship the true and living God to sing from the heart the closing stanza from **William Cowper's** beautiful hymn, *"O, for a Closer Walk":*

"The dearest idol I have known,
Whate'er that idol be,
Help me to tear it from Thy throne,
And worship only Thee."

At the time of the giving of the law the Lord had just demonstrated His supreme power over all other gods by a series of mighty miracles in the deliverance of His people from Egyptian bondage, and He prefaced His commands by reminding Israel of that great fact: *"I am the Lord thy God, which have brought thee out of the land of Egypt, out of the house of bondage. Thou shalt have no other gods before Me."*

The revelation to man of the one true and eternal God, who alone deserves worship and divine honors, is the first and most important of all the articles of the Christian faith. To reveal to man the true and ever-living God is the whole purpose of the Scriptures, the gospel, and the first advent of the Son of God.

SUMMARY OF THE LAW

Just as the decalogue is the summary of the Scriptures, the first commandment is the summary of the whole law. In principle it prohibits all kinds of idolatry and everything in the nature of false worship. Jesus gave a summary of man's whole duty when He said to the tempter who offered Him the dominion of the world for an act of worship, *"Get thee hence, Satan: for it is written, Thou shalt worship the Lord thy God, and Him only shalt thou serve."* Matthew 4:10.

It was idolatry, or false worship, that excluded man from Paradise, and the passport to Paradise restored is the worship of and obedience to the only true God. *"Blessed are they that do His commandments, that they may have right to the tree of life, and may enter in through the gates into the city."* Revelation 22:14.

Because He is the Creator, the supreme right of the Lord in this world is the recognition of His sovereignty and the reverent obedience of His subjects. The first and greatest of all the obligations of man is to his Creator, in whom *"we live, and move, and have our being."* In the first commandment, therefore, is the foundation of the whole law, the basis of all the commands that follow.

The decalogue, like the Lord's prayer, begins at the place of all beginnings-with God. That is where the Bible begins–*"In the beginning God created the heaven and the earth."* The New Testament begins at the same place: *"In the beginning was the Word, and the Word was with God, and the Word was God."* John 1:1. The Gospel of John is just as truly the beginning of the New Testament as is the book of Matthew.

There is no other place to begin, but with God. Jesus declared Himself to be the *"first,"* the *"Alpha,"* the *"beginning,"* and *"the beginning of the creation of God."* On the banks of the Jordan, Moses repeated the first commandment in the words, *"Hear, O Israel: The Lord our God is one Lord."* Deuteronomy 6:4. He then added, *"And thou shalt love the Lord thy God with all thine heart, and with all thy soul, and with all thy might."* Verse 5. It was in these words that Jesus summed up the first table of the decalogue. (See Matthew 22: 36-38.)

The apostle Paul declared that *"we know that an idol is nothing in the world, and that there is none other God but one. For though there be that are called gods, whether in heaven or in earth, (as there be gods many, and lords many,) but to us there is but one God, the Father, of whom are all things, and we in Him; and one Lord Jesus Christ, by whom are all things, and we by Him."* 1 Corinthians 8:4-6.

EVIDENCE OF DIVINITY

The Lord does not leave us without proof of His divinity and supremacy over all other gods. He issues two challenges to false gods, which they are unable to meet. The first and greatest evidence of Deity is the power to create, and Jehovah challenges all other gods to prove their right to be worshiped by exhibiting the power of creation. (See Psalms 95:3, 5, 6; 96: 8-10; 86: 8-10; Isaiah 45:18-22; Jeremiah 10:10-15.)

It is because Jehovah is the Creator that the sinless inhabitants of heaven worship Him. In vision the revelator saw these creatures *"fall down before Him that sat on the throne, and worship Him that liveth forever and ever, and cast their crowns before the throne, saying, Thou art worthy, O Lord, to receive glory and honor and power: for Thou hast created all things, and for Thy pleasure they are and were created."* Revelation 4:10, 11. There is no other true basis of worship. No created being has a right to worship or receive worship from another creature. Since no creature has creative power, the Creator alone is the true and only God.

The Lord also issues another challenge to false gods as a proof of His divinity and the right to command and receive worship, namely, His ability to see and foretell the future. (Isaiah 41: 21-24; 48: 3-6.) Only the members of the Godhead can foresee and forecast future events. All prophecy originates with the Father, and is revealed to man by the Son through the agencies of the Holy Spirit, the angels, and the prophets. (See **1 Peter 1:10, 11; 2 Peter 1:19-21; Revelation 1:1.**)

The angel Gabriel, the most exalted creature in the heavenly host, refused to receive worship from the prophet John, because he himself was likewise a creature. He told him to *"worship God."* (**Revelation 19:10.**) Paul and Barnabas indignantly refused worship and divine honors from the people of Lystra because of a miracle they had performed in their midst. *"They rent their clothes, and ran in among the people, crying out, and saying, Sirs, why do ye these things? We also are men of like passions with you, and preach unto you that ye should turn from these vanities unto the living God, which made heaven, and earth, and the sea, and all things that are therein."* **Acts 14:14, 15.** In accepting worship, Satan or any of his followers exalt themselves to the place of God.

POLYTHEISM CONDEMNED

The first command is a condemnation of, and a warning against, polytheism, or the worship of many gods. *"There be gods many, and lords many,"* said Paul. It has been estimated that the Greeks worshiped thirty thousand gods. The Babylonians *"praised the gods of gold, and of silver, of brass, of iron, of wood, and of stone."* **Daniel 5:4.** The gods of the Egyptians were almost innumerable. The Romans had so many gods that in the city of Rome they built a temple called the Pantheon, or the temple of all the gods. They were so numerous that the priests of the temple could not name or enumerate them all. Modern India is said to have more than 330,000,000 gods, and they are almost as numerous in China. The Israelites had just been delivered from a nation where polytheism and pantheism reigned supreme, and from which the Jews were never completely delivered till after their return from Babylonian captivity. The Promised Land was filled with nations that were polytheistic in their worship, and whose gods became a snare to the children of Israel. Polytheism is the religion of the vast majority of the inhabitants of the modern world, and the first commandment of the decalogue is just as applicable and up to date as when given thirty-five hundred years ago. The law of God is universal. It belongs to the whole human race in all ages. Even in countries where idols or graven images are no longer worshiped as such, gods in other forms constitute an idolatry no less displeasing to Jehovah.

IDOLATRY DEFINED

The apostle Paul defines idolatry as the exchanging of *"the truth of God for a lie"* and the worshiping and serving of *"the creature rather than the Creator"* (**Romans 1:25**, R. V.), or *"more than the Creator."* *"They had bartered the reality of God for what is unreal, and had offered divine honors and religious service to created things, rather than to the Creator,"* is the Weymouth translation. In other words idolatry in its broad meaning is false worship of every kind. Any object of adoration and worship that takes the place of God or comes between us and God is an idol.

Creature worship is just as popular and universal now as when paganism reigned supreme. It began at the dawn of human history when man first sinned. Adam set up an idol in his heart when he served and obeyed Satan instead of the Creator by eating of the forbidden fruit. That was the beginning of idolatry and false worship in the earth. Self and Satan took the place of God. Creature worship supplanted Creator worship.

Idolatry in many forms became prevalent among the descendants of Adam and Eve. It was the great sin of the antediluvian world. It was reintroduced after the deluge by the great rebel Nimrod. Babylon became the cradle of an idolatrous and spurious worship that has come down to modern times. The counterfeit religion of Satan is still divinely called *"Babylon the Great, the Mother of Harlots and Abomination of the Earth."* Revelation 17:5.

MODERN IDOLATRY

For the vast majority of earth's inhabitants there has been no change in the forms of pagan idolatry. The same gods without change even in names are being worshiped in heathen and pagan lands. In countries influenced by the gospel the old gods are still present but in different forms and under new names. The only graven images known to many of us are those seen in museums or exhibited by missionaries returned from heathen lands. There is not the least danger of our worshiping images in these forms of gross idolatry, but the devil is cunning and deceptive. He has hidden the identity of the old gods in new and more attractive garments, and they are worshiped with as much fervor and devotion as were the gods in days of yore.

The instinct to worship was divinely planted in human nature. It is not even necessary to command worship, for all races of mankind, whether their civilization be high or low, have had deities and forms of worship. Voltaire declared that *"if there were no God, it would be necessary to invent Him."* And Theodore Parker truthfully said, *"Yet, if he would, man cannot live all to this world. If not religious, he will be superstitious. If he worship not the true God, he will have his idols."* Job recognized the universal instinct to worship and the inherent principle of idolatry in fallen man when he said: *"If I have made gold my hope, or have said to the fine gold, Thou art my confidence; if I rejoiced because my wealth was great, and because mine hand had gotten much; if I beheld the sun when it shined, or the moon walking in brightness; and my heart hath been secretly enticed, or my mouth hath kissed my hand: this also was an iniquity to be punished by the judge: for I should have denied the God that is above."* Job 31: 24-28.

In this text gold and wealth in which men trust is reckoned as idolatry, along with the worship of the heavenly bodies. The god of gold is one of the chief gods of modern idolatry. The ancient name of this god was *"Mammon,"* and Jesus declared, *"Ye cannot serve God and Mammon."*

Today the rule of gold is more powerful than the golden rule in the lives of the majority of human beings.

The Lord is *"a jealous God"* who refuses to share worship with any other god. The worship of the true God cannot be mixed with the worship of false gods. An ancient proverb declares that *"when the half-gods go, the gods arrive."* When we dismiss all the lesser gods, the great God Himself arrives to claim our allegiance and worship. With Him it is all or none. He accepts no halfhearted service. We must seek and serve Him with all the heart. The promise is, *"The Lord is with you, while ye be with Him; and if ye seek Him, He will be found of you; but if ye forsake Him, He will forsake you."* 2 Chronicles 15:2. We are then told that the Jews *"sought Him with their whole desire; and He was found of them: and the Lord gave them rest round about."* Verse 15. Jesus laid down the same principle when He said, *"He that is not with Me is against Me; and he that gathereth not with Me scattereth abroad."* Matthew 12:30.

29

One writer has recently said:

> "We of today do not believe in these lesser gods. But in spite of that fact, we are as truly polytheists as they. We no longer think of Mars as a person, but we worship the things for which he stood with the same loyal devotion of those of the long ago. We no longer bow at the shrine of Venus, but that for which Venus stood still lays its enslaving and defiling hand on millions. We would never dream of worshiping Bacchus, the god of drink and revelry, as a person. But perhaps he has never been shown greater respect, nor had more willing worshipers, than in wet America today."
> –CLOVIS G. CHAPPELL, *Ten Rules for Living*, p. 22.

Some of the forms of modern idolatry have been aptly stated by another writer:

> "While spurning gods plural and poor, and while acknowledging the sole superlative Jehovah, man may be, and often is, offering only a divided allegiance, a partial worship, to the one true God. What, for example, though we know and assert that there is no such being as Bacchus, if we put ourselves under bondage to that of which Bacchus of classical lore was the acknowledged deity, and become slaves to dissipation, in one or other of its many forms? What matters it, if Plutus, in mythological person, is discredited and disowned by us, if, on the other hand, we are actual, or even would-be, worshipers in the temple of Mammon, which is prominent, if not pre-eminent, in the life and interest of today? If we have long ago deposed Hygeia, the goddess of health, from her godhead, do we not all today worship at the shrine of Hygiene? Nay, do some of us accord more reverence and service to the cause of bodily health than we do to that of the welfare and peace of the soul?"
> –JOHN BURR,
> **Studies on the Ten Commandments**, pp. 17, 18.

AN UP-TO-DATE LAW

The first commandment, as well as the other nine, is as up to date now as when first spoken. It is indeed strange that some believe and even teach that this great code of morals was set aside by Christ. Some of the Jews accused Christ of this purpose, for which He gave them the following severe rebuke: *"Think not that I am come to destroy the law or the prophets: I am not come to destroy, but to fulfill. For verily I say unto you, Till heaven and earth pass, one jot or one tittle shall in no wise pass from the law, till all be fulfilled. Whosoever therefore shall break one of these least commandments, and shall teach men so, he shall be called the least in the kingdom of heaven: but whosoever shall do and teach them, the same shall be called great in the kingdom of heaven."* Matthew 5:17-19.

This statement precludes the possibility of even *"the least"* of these ten commands becoming obsolete or being eliminated from the decalogue. It goes still further and declares that not even *"one jot or one tittle"*–the dot over an "i" or the cross of a "t"–will ever *"pass from the law."* Jesus declared that the smallest people in the estimation of the inhabitants of the universe are those who break even the least of them and that the man who teaches others to transgress is a little man engaged in little business. On the other hand, the truly great in this world are those who carefully obey every command and by precept and example lead others to loyalty to Jehovah by living in harmony with the fundamental law of His kingdom.

Speaking of the first of the ten commandments, **Ferdinand S. Schenck** said:

> *"It is claimed by some that the Lord Jesus Christ has abolished the ten commandments. On the contrary Christ claims that He came not to destroy but to fulfill the law. The law can give no ability to keep it-that is not its province. It shows the rule of duty, awakens the conscience, holds before us God's lofty ideal, incites all the power within us to highest action; but there its mission ends. It evokes all the power within, but confers no power from without.... Christ abolish this commandment! and God no longer claim the highest place in man's thoughts and affections! No, never! Man may degrade himself, but God will never degrade him. Christ came bringing divine power to restore*

man from degradation to the high nobility of keeping this commandment. His glorious work is not to set it aside, but to re-establish it as the rule of life to all His followers."
— *The Ten Commandments and the Lord's Prayer,*
pp. 24, 25.

Not only a return to religion, but a return to the worship of the only true and living God is the demand of the gospel and the call of the hour. *"This is life eternal, that they might know Thee, the only true God, and Jesus Christ, whom Thou hast sent,"* were the words of Jesus in His prayer to the Father as recorded in **John 17:3.** This is the very essence of true knowledge, the acme of real education, and to seek for it should be our first work.

THE TRUE MODE
OF WORSHIP

3

"*Thou shalt not make unto thee any graven image, or any likeness of anything that is in heaven above, or that is in the earth beneath, or that is in the water under the earth: thou shalt not bow down thyself to them, nor serve them: for I the Lord thy God am a jealous God, visiting the iniquity of the fathers upon the children unto the third and fourth generation of them that hate Me; and showing mercy unto thousands of them that love Me, and keep My commandments.*" Exodus 20: 4-6.

While the first and second commandments of the decalogue are closely related in that they both prohibit idolatry and false worship, there is, nevertheless, a distinct difference between them. The first deals with the question of who is the true God, and the second, of how He shall be worshiped. The second is not a repetition of the first as some believe. The distinction is as great as that which exists between any of the other ten. The first commandment reveals the true object of worship; and the second, the true mode of worship. The first tells us who alone must be worshiped, and the second tells us how He must be worshiped, or how He must not be worshiped. The first prohibits false gods; the second forbids false forms of worship.

The first commandment deals with our conception of God; the second, with our external acts as manifested in worship. The second is directed against the false worship of the true God. He must not be worshiped through idols or images or any other visible manifestations. We must not forget that the negative always implies the positive. Prohibited false gods and false worship presupposed a

33

true God and a true mode of worship, and forbidden sins always involve commanded duties. The negative command, *"Thou shalt not,"* always implies the positive command, *"Thou shalt."* Iniquity forbidden indicates righteousness commanded. The command, *"Thou shalt have no other gods before Me,"* implies the command, *"Thou shalt worship the Lord thy God, and Him only shalt thou serve."*

SPIRITUAL WORSHIP

Both internal belief and external acts are involved in worship, and these are distinguished by the first two commandments. The outward acts of worship reveal the thoughts and intents of the heart. As a man *"thinketh in his heart, so is he"* in conduct. The distinction between false gods and false forms of worship must be recognized, for counterfeit methods of worshiping even the true God are a dangerous species of idolatry.

We are told that spiritual things are spiritually discerned. (1 Corinthians 2:14.) It is therefore impossible to portray spiritual things through material images or representations. To the woman at the well in Samaria, Jesus said, *"God is a Spirit: and they that worship Him must worship Him in spirit and in truth."* John 4:24. The prohibiting of bodily prostrations to visible gods or idols presupposes the spiritual worship of the invisible God. To attempt to substitute a visible image of a created object for the invisible Creator Himself would be as foolish as substituting the light of a candle for the light of the sun. Jesus said to the woman, *"The hour cometh, and now is, when the true worshipers shall worship the Father in spirit and in truth: for the Father seeketh such to worship Him."* John 4:23. This is the spiritual worship demanded in the second commandment. True worship is far more than religious forms and ceremonies. Worship is always perverted and degraded by those who become fully occupied with externals and substitute them for spiritual experience. The vision of the Christian must transcend things material and behold the spiritual, and like Moses be able to endure, *"as seeing Him who is invisible."* Hebrews 11:27.

GRAVEN IMAGES

The second commandment first of all forbids the making of images or likenesses of any created object in heaven or earth for the purpose of worship. That it does not prohibit pictures in the form of paintings, engravings, photographs, or statues for other purposes than worship is evident from the fact that the Lord, soon after this command was given, directed Moses to make such likenesses in connection with the building of the sanctuary. Moses was commanded to make engraved and embroidered figures of angels, oxen, lions, trees, fruits, and flowers. When he erected the temple at Jerusalem under divine direction, Solomon declared that *"he carved all the walls of the house round about with carved figures of cherubims and palm trees and open flowers within and without."* 1 Kings 6:29.

In 1 Kings 7:29 we are told that there were statues of *"lions, oxen, and cherubims."* The tabernacle and temple were both built under divine direction, and we can be sure that the Lord would never transgress His own command or compel His people to do so. At a later time the Lord directed Moses to make the likeness of a serpent and set it up in the camp of Israel. Seven centuries later when this brazen serpent was venerated as an object of worship, King Hezekiah had it destroyed. (2 Kings 18:3-7.) Everything depends on the motive or purpose for which the likeness is made. The fact that the Jews have never been given to painting or sculpturing is no argument against these arts or an excuse for such extreme and fanatical positions taken by some professed Christians. The work of human hands is not forbidden by the second commandment. The prohibition has to do only with the worship of that work. Only when the work becomes the object of worship is it idolatry.

The injunction, *"My little children, guard yourselves from idols,"* was written, not to the image-worshiping heathen, but to Christians. The most dangerous forms of idolatry are not easily discernible. A superstitious reverence for the forms, ceremonies, and ordinances of religion may lead to idolatry. The worshiper who trusts in baptism as a means of salvation rather than as an outward sign of an inward cleansing has made this ordinance an idol. Likewise he who looks to the bread and wine of the communion service rather than to that which it represents, is an idolater. To make saving acts of religious symbols is to transform them into idols.

CREATURE WORSHIP

An idol is any creature or created thing put in the place of God. Idolatry is creature rather than Creator worship, and of all forms of idolatry the most degraded and senseless is the worship of the mere image of the genuine. A man is always superior to what he makes, and in worshiping the works of his own hands he is worshiping that which is below and inferior to himself. Image worship is even inferior to the worship of what God has made. But a picture or image even of God, if such a thing were possible, would of necessity degrade our conception of Him.

To make sure that man can never make an imitation or likeness of God, He has made Himself invisible to man and has never permitted him to behold His person. It is therefore impossible to produce a picture, engraving, or statue of the Creator. On the banks of the Jordan, Moses gave a detailed explanation of the second commandment, in which he reminded the children of Israel that when the law was given on Mount Sinai they saw no similitude of the Lawgiver: *"Take ye therefore good heed unto yourselves; for ye saw no manner of similitude on the day that the Lord spake unto you in Horeb out of the midst of the fire."* Deuteronomy 4:15. This is one of the reasons why *"no man hath seen God at any time."*

If God had at any time displayed His person to man, idolatry would have been much worse. It is for this same reason that Christ left no painting or even word picture of Himself by which we may know what He looked like. Our pictures of Him are of very doubtful origin. They are simply the product of human imagination and doubtless bear but little or no resemblance to His appearance during His earthly sojourn. The prophet declared that when He would come into the world there would be *"no form nor comeliness; and when we shall see Him, there is no beauty that we should desire Him."* Isaiah 53:2.

When the law was given, the Israelites had just been delivered from one of the worst forms of pagan idolatry and were about to enter a land filled with idols and idolatry. In both Egypt and Canaan polytheism and pantheism reigned supreme. The Egyptians worshiped "the likeness of male and female." Osiris and his wife, Isis, were the chief Egyptian divinities. All heathen gods were men and women in their originals. After their death they were deified and worshiped, and still are, under various names.

In Egypt the ox and the heifer were objects of worship, as were also the stork, crane, hawk, crocodile, serpent, frog, and the fish of the river Nile. Every living thing was a god, and God was in every living thing. Within forty days after receiving the law with its prohibitions of idolatry, the Israelites made and worshiped a golden calf, demonstrating the instability and untrustworthiness of human nature. The golden calf was probably never intended to represent a false god, but was their conception of the image of Jehovah, who had brought them out of the land of Egypt. Aaron said to them, *"These be thy gods, O Israel, which brought thee up out of the land of Egypt."* **Exodus 32:4.** The next day Aaron proclaimed *"a feast to the Lord"* or *"to Jehovah."* (American Revised Version.) They had not seen *"any manner of similitude"* of Jehovah, and feeling that they must have some visible representation of Him, they made one after the manner of one of the gods of Egypt with which they were so familiar.

HEATHEN CLAIMS

The most enlightened heathen have always claimed that they did not worship the idol or image itself, but the being or power dwelling in or represented by it. This was doubtless the conception of Aaron and the Israelites at the base of Mount Sinai. They probably had no idea of deliberately worshiping a false god, but Jehovah, through a visible symbol of Him. That this is the pagan idea of worship is evident from the following:

> *"We worship the gods... through the images."* *"We do not consider materials of brass, silver, or other things of which the statues are made, to be themselves gods, or sacred divinities, but in these materials we worship and venerate the gods whom the holy dedication brings in and causes to dwell in the images wrought by the craftsman."*
>
> –ARNOBIUS,
> ***Against the Heathen**, Book 6, Chaps. 9, 17.*
> (Arnobius lived near the close of the third century A.D.)

Another pagan said:

> *"Visible and tangible images are, as it were, only the bodies of the gods, and that there dwelt in them certain spirits, which have been invited to come into them, and which have power to inflict harm, or to fulfill the desires of those by whom divine honors and services are rendered them."*
>
> –HERMES TRISMEGISTUS, quoted by AUGUSTINE

This is also the position of the Greek and Roman Catholics in regard to the images of Christ, angels, and saints. They claim that they do not worship the images themselves, but what they represent. But this is also clearly forbidden in the second commandment. *"Thou shalt not bow down thyself to them, nor serve them,"* is a condemnation of Catholic practices, and for this reason the second commandment is eliminated from most of their writings, even though it is found in the Latin Vulgate which is considered by Roman Catholics to be even more authentic than the original Scriptures themselves.

WORSHIP OF THE DEAD

The worship of images is really the worship of dead and deified men and women who after death supposedly became gods or "as gods." All graven images represent dead heroes, ancestors, or saints. At its root idolatry is ancestor worship.

> *"Sun worship and nature worship constituted the essence of the pagan system; but there is, nevertheless, the strongest evidence to show that the first originals of the pagan gods were men who after death were deified; that this was the real foundation of the pagan system; and that these spirits of the dead, according to their different attributes, were subsequently identified with the sun, moon and stars, etc., which were regarded as their habitations."*
> –J. GARNIER, *The Worship of the Dead*, p. 13.

Hesiod, a contemporary of **Homer**, said:

> *"The gods were holy men, and the sun, moon, stars were regarded as intelligences because they were the abode of deified men." "The gods were the souls of men who were afterwards worshiped by their posterity, on account of their extraordinary virtues."*
> –FABER, *Origin of Pagan Idolatry, Vol. II*, pp. 224, 227.

This is also the basis for the worship and veneration of saints by Roman Catholics.

Plutarch states that the Egyptian priests taught:

> *"...that Cronus, Osirus, Horus, and all their other principal deities were once mere men, but that after they died their souls migrated into some one or other of the heavenly bodies, and became the animating spirits of their new celestial mansions."*
> —*De Iside*, p. 354.

Cicero declared that:

> *"...the initiated (into the pagan mysteries) must know that they worshiped men's souls departed from their bodies into heaven, and that all heaven was filled with men."*
> —BISHOP CUMBERLAND,
> *Tully & Tusculam Questions,* p. 349.

This is the origin of the saying that a person "has found his place in the sun."

DEMON WORSHIP

Since the dead are unconscious and *"know not anything"* and have nothing whatever to do with *"anything that is done under the sun"* (**Ecclesiastes 9: 5, 6**), and the pretended spirits of the dead are really the spirits of devils, or evil angels, impersonating the dead for the purpose of deception, the worship of idols constitutes demon worship and is so designated in the Scriptures. Moses told the Israelites that they *"shall no more offer their sacrifices unto devils, after whom they have gone a whoring."* **Leviticus 17: 7.** He also said: *"They provoked Him to jealousy with strange gods, with abominations provoke they Him to anger. They sacrificed unto devils, not to God; to gods whom they knew not, to new gods that came newly up, whom your fathers feared not. Of the Rock that begat thee thou art unmindful, and hast forgotten God that formed thee."* **Deuteronomy 32:16-18.**

In **Psalms 106:36-38** we are told that the children of Israel *"served their idols: which were a snare unto them"* and *"they sacrificed their sons and their daughters unto devils"* when they *"sacrificed unto the idols of Canaan."* In **verse 28** we are told that the Israelites *"joined themselves also unto Baalpeor, and ate the* *sacrifices of the dead."* The apostle Paul declared that the pagan Gentiles *"sacrifice to devils, and not to God."* **1 Corinthians 10: 20.** This explains why idol worship is such an abomination unto the Lord. In reality it is the worship of Satan, *"the god of this world,"* which is creature worship of the worst type. How true it is that *"the whole world lies in the power of the evil one."* Idolatry is Satan's effort to substantiate his first lie to Adam and Eve when he said, *"Ye shall not surely die: for God doth know that in the day ye eat thereof, then your eyes shall be opened, and ye shall be as gods, knowing good and evil."* Genesis 3: 4, 5. He is still saying that the dead are not surely dead, but are gods, or as gods. The majority of mankind believe this lie. The belief in the immortality of the soul is almost universal. This is the very essence of paganism and the foundation of demon worship.

THE GREAT APOSTASY

The great apostasy, or "falling away" from the apostolic faith, during the early Christian centuries was a return to heathen idolatry under the disguise of a Christian exterior. The apostles were scarcely dead before the early Christians began to make images of them and venerate relics of apostolic days. This apostasy ripened into its full fruitage between the fourth and eighth centuries. The historian **Gibbon** says of this change in the form of the Christian religion:

> *"The sublime and simple theology of the primitive Christians was gradually corrupted; and the monarchy of heaven, already clouded by metaphysical subtleties, was degraded by the introduction of a popular mythology, which tended to restore the reign of polytheism."*
> –**EDWARD GIBBON,** *History of the Decline and Fall of the Roman Empire. Vol. II,* chap. 28, p. 619.

> *"The first introduction of a symbolic worship was in the veneration of the cross, and of relics.... At first, the experiment was made with caution and scruple; and the venerable pictures [of saints and martyrs] were discreetly allowed to instruct the ignorant, to awaken the cold, and to gratify the prejudices of the heathen proselytes."* *"Before the end of the sixth century, these images... were the objects of worship, and the instruments of*

miracles." "But in the beginning of the eighth century.... the more timorous Greeks were awakened by an apprehension, that under the mask of Christianity, they had restored the religion of their fathers."

–Id., Vol. IV, Chap. 49, pp. 249, 250, 252, 253.

It seems to be a human instinct to want to worship something visible and tangible. It is so much easier to be carnal than spiritual. This explains the general demand for ritualism on the part of unspiritual people. They seem to feel that a great outward show of religion makes up for the lack of an inward experience. They do not seem to know that *"the things which are seen are temporal; but the things which are not seen are eternal."* 2 Corinthians 4:18. The most lasting and valuable things even of this life are invisible. Love, joy, peace, righteousness, and character cannot be seen, and yet they are more precious and eternal than all the things that are visible to the naked eye. Faith is said to be *"the substance of things hoped for, the evidence of things not seen."* Hebrews 11:1.

A JEALOUS GOD

"For I... am a jealous God," is the reason the Lord gives as to why man should worship Him alone. This is not the kind of jealousy so severely condemned in the Scriptures. This is a just and holy jealousy that is free from sin. Human jealousy is usually based on selfishness. It is characterized by envy and unjust suspicion. It is the result of a lack of trust and confidence. Human jealousy is divinely declared to be *"as cruel as the grave."* *"O jealousy, thou ugliest fiend of hell!"* exclaimed **Hannah More**, and it is described in **Othello** as *"the green-eyed monster which doth mock the meat it feeds on."*

But God's jealousy is the offspring of love. His love for us is so great that He will brook no rivals. He so values our purity and happiness that He threatens to destroy all that would mar them. A father guards and protects his children and a husband his wife with jealous care, because of his love for them. **Dale** spoke of this sort of love when he said that *"jealousy is but the anger and pain of injured and insulted love."*

False gods and false worship wound God's love. The original word for jealousy indicates the jealousy of a husband for the purity of his wife, whom he loves with an affection that will tolerate no

41

rival. All through the Scriptures the relationship between God and His people is represented by the marriage union, which is the sweetest and most intimate human relationship known. The violation of this relationship is the greatest of all human trespasses. It is for this reason that idolatry is so displeasing to God. All through the Scriptures it is designated spiritual fornication and adultery.

PENALTY AND PROMISE

The second commandment is enforced by a threatened penalty and sustained by a precious promise: *"I the Lord thy God am a jealous God, visiting the iniquity of the fathers upon the children unto the third and fourth generation of them that hate Me; and showing mercy unto thousands of them that love Me and keep My commandments."*

This is not an arbitrary decree. It is the unalterable and eternal law of heredity and environment that the sins and faults of the parents are handed down to their children. It is the way of life, and it is foolish to question its justice. "They enslave their children's children who make a compromise with sin," is a true saying. That the parents' traits and tendencies are transmitted to their posterity is a well-known law of science. It is not guesswork. It is a scientific fact.

Most of the sins of children were also the sins of their parents, grandparents, and great-grandparents. This commandment does not mean that the Lord will punish children for the iniquities of their parents, for we are plainly told that *"the son shall not bear the iniquity of the father, neither shall the father bear the iniquity of the son."* Ezekiel 18:20. In Jeremiah 31:30 we are told that each sinner *"shall die for his own iniquity."* (See also 2 Chronicles 25:4.)

It is an unfailing rule of justice that the iniquities of the parents are visited upon their children if they follow in their footsteps, and they usually do. *"As is the mother, so is her daughter,"* is a Biblical proverb recorded in Ezekiel 16:44. Sin is very contagious. But in this commandment it is especially the sin of idolatry that is handed down to future generations. Our characters are largely determined by our religion and the nature of our worship. The parents' ideas of religion are usually accepted by their children. It is a terrible thing to pass down to our children a false conception of God; a heritage of false worship. This is the chief cause of the continuation and perpetuation of evil. It is usually inherited.

REWARD OF OBEDIENCE

The reward of obedience reaches to "a thousand generations." If sin is contagious, virtue and goodness are also. While disobedience descends to the third and fourth generation, the blessed results of obedience reach to the thousandth generation. This is the way of saying they are eternal. Iniquity will eventually run its course and become extinct, but virtue and loyalty will, never die.

Obedience to God's laws, moral and natural, bring a rich reward in character and happiness. On the banks of the Jordan, Moses said to the Israelites, *"Know therefore that the Lord thy God, He is God, the faithful God, which keepeth covenant and mercy with them that love Him and keep His commandments to a thousand generations."* Deuteronomy 7: 9. Wrath and divine judgments are spoken of as God's *"strange work"* (Isaiah 28: 21), but He *"pardoneth iniquity, and passeth by the transgression of the remnant of His heritage. He retaineth not His anger forever, because He delighteth in mercy."* Micah 7:18.

"The third and fourth generation" indicates a limit to God's wrath, but *"a thousand generations"* shows that God's love and mercy are unlimited. His mercy far outweighs His justice. His justice is great, but His mercy is greater. His mercy reaches far beyond His wrath. Men may criticize God's justice as set forth in this commandment, but they never object to the benefits they inherit from their ancestors. We are constantly reaping a golden harvest of character and conduct from the seed-sowing of previous generations.

The second commandment suggests that:

"...the righteousness of men endures longer than their sin. 'The third and fourth generation' may suffer the penalty of great crimes; but thousands of generations cannot wholly exhaust the reward of fidelity to God and obedience to His commandments. The evil which comes from man's wickedness endures for a time,

43

but perishes at last; the good that comes from man's well-doing is all but indestructible."
–R. W. DALE, *The Ten Commandments,* p. 57.

The righteousness of God, which is imputed and imparted to His people, is called "an everlasting righteousness." It will endure through all eternity.

LESSON FOR PARENTS

In this threat and promise is a warning to parents. The evils they transmit to their children in character, example, conduct, and disease, will endure through several generations. What a fearful responsibility this places upon them. On the other hand, the goodness, virtue, and righteousness they instill in their children's characters through precept and example, will continue in their posterity through all coming time and eternity. Those who love and obey God will be rewarded with the life that is "more abundant" in the kingdom that will never end. There will be no limit to their existence and happiness.

The psalmist said: *"Evildoers shall be cut off: but those that wait upon the Lord, they shall inherit the earth. For yet a little while, and the wicked shall not be: yea, thou shalt diligently consider his place, and it shall not be. But the meek shall inherit the earth; and shall delight themselves in the abundance of peace."* Psalms 37: 9-11.

This is another way of expressing the threat and promise of the second commandment. The promise of mercy extends to all generations of those who love and obey the Lord. We must love God before we can keep His commandments, for *"love is the fulfilling of the law."* **Romans 13:10.** Jesus said, *"If ye love Me, keep My commandments,"* and the apostle John declared, *"This is the love of God, that we keep His commandments; and His commandments are not grievous."* 1 John 5:3.

THE GODS OF
MODERN IDOLATRY

4

"*What agreement hath the temple of God with idols? for ye are the temple of the living God; as God hath said, I will dwell in them, and walk in them; and I will be their God, and they shall be My people.*" 2 Corinthians 6:16.

The temple here mentioned is not a pagan temple filled with graven images. It is the temple of the soul, and the false gods are the idols of the heart. The message is addressed not to image-worshiping pagans but to professed Christians. The heart or heart-temple should have no agreement or covenant with idols. These gods of modern idolatry are just as defiling as were those that polluted the temple at Jerusalem during the reigns of Judah's most wicked kings. The Lord returned to His temple when it was cleansed of idols, and He was recognized and worshiped as the only true God. The holy God will dwell only in a holy temple.

Again the apostle Paul wrote: "*Know ye not that ye are the temple of God, and that the Spirit of God dwelleth in you? If any man defile the temple of God, him shall God destroy; for the temple of God is holy, which temple ye are.*" 1 Corinthians 3:16, 17. Idolatry defiles the heart-temple, and unless it is cleansed of its unholy traffic, it must be destroyed. There is no other way, for God will not tolerate idolatry in any form.

MODERN GODS

Because idolatry in its gross forms, as practiced in heathen lands, is practically unknown in America, many professed Christians have feelings of complacency and self-satisfaction. Like the proud and self-righteous Pharisee in the temple, they thank God that they are not like other men, and especially the idol-worshiping heathen. They forget that there are many kinds of idols and many forms of idolatry, and that one is just as much an abomination to God as the other. Refined idolatry is just as displeasing to God as gross idolatry. It is to us that the admonition is given, *"Little children, keep yourselves from idols."* 1 John 3:21.

Idolatry is the serving and worshiping of *"the creature more than the Creator."* Romans 1: 25. *"Creature"* includes everything that has been created. Whatever we love most and make the most of is a god. Whatever or whoever we love and serve "more than" the Creator is an idol. We may even love and worship the Creator, but if we love something or someone more than we do Him, we are guilty of idolatry according to the divinely inspired definition. On this basis there are as many false gods in one of our large American cities as in ancient Athens or Rome. When Paul visited Athens, *"his spirit was stirred in him, when he saw the city wholly given to idolatry"* (Acts 17:16), or *"full of idols"* (margin). His feelings would be similar were he to visit New York or Chicago today. The difference in the forms of idolatry would not deceive him in the least.

THE DECALOGUE

The first two commands of the decalogue forbid all kinds of idolatry in every age, including our own. In the first the Lord demands that He alone be worshiped, and in the second we are commanded to come directly to Him with no image, similitude, or creature between. It forbids the making of anything that represents Him, including an image of Him or any of His creatures, to assist man in his worship. The second commandment demands that we worship God directly without anything or any creature between. To permit a priest or ritual or even a religion to come between us and God is the very essence of idolatry. To make saving acts of religious forms and ceremonies is to transform them into idols.

Ritualism and ascetic worship never increase spirituality and easily become a species of idolatry. Those who claim to worship God through nature often become worshipers of nature itself. This form of creature worship is known as pantheism. Modern science has made idolatry more sinful than ever. By the explanation of many of the phenomena of nature on the basis of natural law, many of the reasons for idolatry have been removed, and its continuance is therefore inexcusable. The marvelous discoveries of modern science, however, have increased the worship of human works. The exaltation and deification of human achievements -the worship of the works of our own hands-presents a god before which millions bow in reverence and admiration in this age of invention, discovery, and scientific progress. Speaking of "the last days," the prophet says, *"Their land also is full of idols; they worship the work of their own hands, that which their own fingers have made."* Isaiah 2:2, 8.

PERVERTED REASON

Paul declared that the idolaters of his day *"became vain in their imaginations, and their foolish heart was darkened. Professing themselves to be wise, they became fools."* Romans 1:21, 22. The exaltation of the human intellect dethrones God. Satan promised Adam and Eve that if they disobeyed the word of God and made up their own minds through the power of human reasoning, they would *"be as gods."* Perverted reason has been one of the ruling gods of the human family ever since.

When the French revolutionists attempted to destroy the knowledge and worship of the true God, knowing that man must have something to worship, they exalted in His place the Goddess of Reason. Placing this false goddess on the altar, the idolaters of Paris and other parts of France gave divine honors to human intellect rather than to Him who is *"infinite in wisdom"* and *"in whom are hid all the treasures of wisdom and knowledge."*

Today men do not worship perverted reason in the same gross fashion, but nevertheless the materialistic philosophy of the twentieth century dethrones the Creator, the God of the Bible, and deifies human reason in His stead. The heady and high-minded spirit of the modern world has exalted the human will above the authority of the Scriptures. The idolatry of human opinion is leading millions to deny the claims of God as revealed in His Word.

47

The person who exalts his own word above the Word of God, and his own will above the will of God, is an idolater. The person who believes that the conclusion of human reasoning is an answer to prayer makes his own mind his god and is an idolater of the pantheistic type.

THE WORSHIP OF SELF

The following is a divinely inspired picture of our own generation: *"This know also, that in the last days perilous times shall come. For men shall be lovers of their own selves, covetous, boasters, proud, blasphemers, disobedient to parents, unthankful, unholy, without natural affection, trucebreakers, false accusers, incontinent, fierce, despisers of those that are good, traitors, heady, high-minded, lovers of pleasures more than lovers of God; having a form of godliness, but denying the power thereof: from such turn away."* 2 Timothy 3:1-5.

Here is a graphic description of modern idolatry. Self-love always leads to self-worship and to the other sins here enumerated. Self is the creature that is worshiped above all others. Selfishness is the first fruit of all the works of the flesh, just as true love is the first fruit of the spiritual harvest. The exaltation of self to the place of God began with Lucifer. The question is asked, *"How art thou fallen from heaven, O Lucifer, son of the morning! how art thou cut down to the ground, which didst weaken the nations!"* The answer is: *"Thou hast said in thine heart, I will ascend into heaven, I will exalt my throne above the stars of God: I will sit also upon the mount of the congregation, in the sides of the north: I will ascend above the heights of the clouds; I will be like the Most High. Yet thou shalt be brought down to hell, to the sides of the pit."* Isaiah 14:12-15.

After the fall of man Satan became *"the god of this world,"* whose worship is almost universal. This is the very center of all creature worship or idolatry. In worshiping self we really worship Satan. We become antichrists when we permit the spirit of Satan to rule our lives so that we exalt self to the place of God. Paul warned of the *"falling away"* when *"that man of sin"* would *"be revealed, the son of perdition; who opposeth and exalteth himself above all that is called God, or that is worshiped; so that he as God sitteth in the temple of God, showing himself that he is God."* 2 Thessalonians 2:3, 4.

48

"This is that spirit of antichrist" mentioned in 1 John 4:1-4, and in *1 John 2:18* we are told that in *"the last time"* there would be *"many antichrists."* An antichrist is any person who manifests an anti-Christian spirit. Christ was the very embodiment of humility. Pride and haughtiness are a satanic spirit. Self-idolatry lies at the foundation of all sin. Putting self in the place of God and selfish interests in the place of God's service is a universal sin today. *"Perilous times"* have come upon our generation because the majority are *"lovers of self."* They are therefore worshipers of self and human achievements.

THE WORSHIP OF OTHERS

The worship of others as well as self is another form of idolatry. Many parents make gods of their children and devote their lives to serving and obeying them. Many children are indulged and pampered and defended until they become self-centered bigots who expect everybody to bow down to them as did their fond but misguided parents. Jesus said, *"He that loveth father or mother more than Me is not worthy of Me: and he that loveth son or daughter more than Me is not worthy of Me."* Matthew 10: 37.

There is also a so-called love for the opposite sex that is idolatry. It is one of the chief forms of creature worship. The person who loves another creature more than the Creator is an idolater. Love between men and women must be kept subordinate to the love for the Creator.

Infatuation is the counterfeit of love and leads its devotees into a very dangerous species of idolatry. It so completely captivates the mind and affections that God is forgotten or ignored. Under this spell of false worship men and women lose their reason and make fools of themselves.

Many of the modern love songs are virtually hymns of praise to a creature-god. They are filled with terms of worship that are used in the worship of God. Sentimental crooners are the chief soloists in the synagogue of Satan, and jazz is the most popular music of his orchestra. This form of idolatry manifests itself in many ways, sometimes invading the very sanctuary of God.

There are many who attend church only when their preacher-god occupies the pulpit. On one occasion **Thomas K. Beecher** substituted for his famous brother, Henry Ward Beecher, at Plymouth church in Brooklyn. Many curiosity seekers had come expecting to hear the latter. When Thomas appeared in the pulpit, many of the sightseers started for the doors. Thomas raised his hand for attention and then said, *"All those who came here this morning to worship Henry Ward Beecher may now withdraw from the church—all who came to worship God may remain."*

WORSHIPERS OF PLEASURE

Being *"lovers of pleasures more than lovers of God"* is another of the prevailing sins of the last days. It is another species of idolatry. Selfish pleasure is an idol at whose shrine many professed Christians spend more time and money than in the house of God and at the altar of prayer. In this pleasure-mad age multiplied thousands of people live only to satisfy their cravings for fun and frolic. In the parable of the sower the *"pleasures of this life"* are said to be *"the thorns"* that *"choke the Word"* so that it *"becometh unfruitful"* and can *"therefore bring no fruit to perfection."*

Paul describes the *"foolish"* who are "**serving divers lusts and pleasures**" instead of God. (**Titus 3:3.**) Service is a form of worship as indicated by Christ's statement to Satan recorded in **Luke 4:8.**: *"Get thee behind Me, Satan: for it is written, Thou shalt worship the Lord thy God, and Him only shalt thou serve,"* and by Paul's statement recorded in **Romans 6:16**: *"Know ye not, that to whom ye yield yourselves servants to obey, his servants ye are to whom ye obey; whether of sin unto death, or of obedience unto righteousness?"*

Entertainment, amusement, and innocent recreation are proper only when kept in their proper place. They are permissible as a means to an end, but when they are sought as an end in themselves, they become a curse instead of a blessing. When a good time and the discovery of new thrills become the absorbing passions of the soul, recreation is sooner or later turned into dissipation. The only kind of recreation that is permissible to a Christian is that which is of such a quality that it re-creates the mind and body. That is what recreation really means, and unless it does this it is a misnomer. If recreation is not the result of the pleasure indulged, it is evident that the means has been substituted for the end and the purpose of pleasure has become the object of life and is therefore a species of idolatry.

THE GOD OF APPETITE

"Many walk, of whom I have told you often, and now tell you even weeping, that they are the enemies of the cross of Christ: whose end is destruction, whose god is their belly, and whose glory is in their shame, who mind earthly things." Philippians 3:18, 19. *"The end of such men is ruin; for their appetites are their god,"* is the rendering in the Twentieth Century New Testament.

In this text we are plainly told that perverted and uncontrolled appetites constitute idolatry. The abject slavery of the present generation to appetites and passions makes this form of idolatry one of, if not the worst of, all the gods of modern times. The idolatry of appetite embraces in its broad sense all the uncontrolled passions of sinful flesh. It includes not only gluttony in eating and drinking but also the gratification of the sensual passions. Those who worship the god of appetite are declared to be *"enemies of the cross of Christ,"* because by indulging the cravings of the lower nature they *"crucify to themselves the Son of God afresh, and put Him to an open shame."*

Thousands of people are foolishly living to eat rather than eating to live. There is a vast difference between these two principles. It is the difference between a fool and a wise man, an idolater and a Christian. Eating and drinking as a means of health and strength is both wise and sensible. But eating and drinking as an end in itself is a foolish, dangerous, and even a deadly practice. It is gluttony and idolatry. While satisfying the legitimate, normal, and temperate appetite should be a pleasure, the means must never be substituted for the end. Eating and drinking as the means of health is a Christian duty, but as the object of life it is idolatry. The god of appetite was, next to Satan, the first false god worshiped by our first parents, and the means therefore of enslaving the world.

Bacchus, the god of drink and revelry, is more popular today than at any time in human history. A divine woe is pronounced upon those who worship at this shrine: *"Woe unto them that rise up early in the morning, that they may follow strong drink; that continue until night, till wine inflame them! And the harp, and the*

51

viol, the tabret, and pipe, and wine, are in their feasts: but they regard not the work of the LORD, neither consider the operation of His hands." Isaiah 5:11, 12.

Never has this enslaving and degrading god had more willing worshipers than at the present time. Nicotine is another modern god that is, if possible, more popular and deadly than strong drink. At this shrine millions of men, women, boys, and girls are daily and hourly presenting their burnt offerings, whose incense smoke ascends to pollute the air with its poison. The number in this age who refuse to worship the cigarette god are very few. They are considered odd and old-fashioned.

Venus, the goddess of sensuality, is another very popular form of idolatry. We have come to the anti-type of the days of Noah when the earth *"was corrupt before God,"* and *"all flesh had corrupted His way upon the earth,"* and when *"every imagination of the thoughts of his heart was only evil continually."* Genesis 6:5-12. (Matthew 24:37-39.) Sinful human flesh is declared to be *"vile"* and the conversation of man *"filthy"* and *"corrupt."* Licentiousness is one of the prevailing sins of the last days, and at this shrine increasing millions pay their vows.

GODDESS OF FASHION

In its broadest sense fashion embraces worldliness in all its forms. The word means to conform to the prevailing modes, practices, and customs of the world. Anything on which a person sets his affections becomes a god.

Said the apostle, *"Know ye not that the friendship of the world is enmity with God? whosoever therefore will be a friend of the world is the enemy of God."* James 4:4. Any form of worldliness is therefore idolatry.

Worldly fashions have to do chiefly with the garments and ornaments with which the body is clothed and decked. All exhibitions of pride and dress which are contrary to the Word of God constitute a species of idolatry.

Note the following Scriptures: *"I would have the women dress becomingly, with modesty and self-control, not with plaited hair or gold or pearls or costly clothes, but-as befits women making a claim to godliness-with the ornament of good works."* 1 Timothy 2:8, 9, Weymouth translation. *"Your adornment ought not to be a merely outward thing-one of plaiting the hair, putting on jewelry, or wearing beautiful dresses. Instead of that, it should be a new nature within-the imperishable ornament of a gentle and peaceful spirit, which is indeed precious in the sight of God. For in ancient times also this was the way the holy women who set their hopes upon God used to adorn themselves."* 1 **Peter** 3:3-5, Weymouth translation.

If these principles were adhered to, the goddess of fashion would soon lose her devotees.

Many professed Christians are wearing graven images on their bodies and do not know it. In paganism in all its forms, disks, circles, and globes have always been the emblems of divinity and eternity. The first of all created objects to be worshiped were the sun, moon, and stars, and they have been the chief gods of the pagan world ever since. Images were made to them in the form of disks, globes, and circles made of gold, silver, brass, precious stones, and other glittering metals resembling the form and brightness of the heavenly bodies which they worshiped. These images of the gods were fastened to the bodies of the worshipers for protection and safe keeping. This is the origin of the wearing of ornaments. All jewelry for the purpose of adornment has its origin in the images of pagan gods.

The second commandment forbids the making of *"any likeness of anything that is in heaven above,"* and is therefore a prohibition of rings, bracelets, and beads for adornment purposes. Aside from the Greek and Roman Catholic images of Christ and the angels, these shining ornaments are the only likenesses of things in the heavens above that could possibly be embraced in this divine restriction.

The more heathen and uncivilized a people are, the more trinkets they put on their bodies, and the more Christian and civilized they become, the less they adorn themselves. The genuine Christian discards all these images to pagan gods and substitutes for them *"the ornament of a meek and quiet spirit, which is in the sight of God of great price."* Jewelry has a bad origin, and those who deck themselves with these useless ornaments are guilty of idolatry. They transgress the first two commandments and the many scriptures which prohibit their use.

53

THE WORSHIP OF MAMMON

"No man can serve two masters: for either he will hate the one and love the other; or else will hold to the one, and despise the other. Ye cannot serve God and mammon." **Matthew 6:24.** *"Mammon"* is an Arabic word for *"wealth."* It represents the god of riches. *"You cannot be bondservants of both God and gold,"* is the Weymouth translation. Paul declares that a *"covetous man"* is *"an idolater,"* and that *"covetousness"* is *"idolatry."* (**Ephesians 5:5; Colossians 3:5.**) Covetousness dethrones God and puts in His stead that which we are determined to have.

Not money, but *"the love of money is the root of all evil."* This is what makes it a species of idolatry. Idolatry is defined as *"inordinate love or admiration."* When money is properly used it is a great blessing. But it must be used as a means, and should never be made the end. As a servant it is valuable, but as a master it is a tyrant. When material things are permitted to hide the Giver, they become idols. **Martin Luther** said, *"That upon which you set your heart, and in which you trust is properly your god."*

Notice again the statement of the patriarch Job: *"If I have made gold my hope, or have said to the fine gold, Thou art my confidence; if I rejoiced because my wealth was great, and because mine hand had gotten much; if I beheld the sun when it shined, or the moon walking in brightness; and my heart hath been secretly enticed, or my mouth hath kissed my hand: this also was an iniquity to be punished by the judge: for I should have denied the God that is above."* Job 31: 24-28. Placing our confidence in "uncertain riches" is here declared to be as verily idolatry as the worship of the sun and moon.

PERMISSIBLE IMAGE WORSHIP

But there is one form of image worship that is not only divinely permitted but actually commanded as the only means of salvation. Because the Father knew that it is difficult for man to worship an invisible God, He sent His Son into the world to become *"Immanuel"* or *"God with us."* The incarnation of the Son of God was *"God manifest in the flesh."* Christ was declared to be *"the image of the invisible God"* and *"the express image of His person."*

54

A graven image cannot be made of Christ, for we have no true picture of Him. But His character is described, and this He has promised to reproduce in us. While character can be imitated, it cannot be sculptured or made into an image. The chief ambition of a Christian should be to worship the only true image of the invisible God and have that image or likeness reproduced. This form of image worship is not idolatry. It is Christianity.

"We all, with open face beholding as in a glass the glory of the Lord, are changed into the same image from glory to glory even as by the Spirit of the Lord." 2 **Corinthians** 3:18. This is the image adoration that transforms character, and all such did the Lord *"predestinate to be conformed to the image of His Son."*

PROFANITY AND
VAIN WORSHIP

5

"Thou shalt not take the name of the LORD thy God in vain; for the LORD will not hold him guiltless that taketh His name in vain." Exodus 20:7. "You shall not use the name of the Eternal, your God, profanely," is the James Moffatt translation. The third commandment of the decalogue is a warning against profanity, falsehood, irreverence, and hypocrisy. It prohibits all forms of vain worship.

In these prohibitions the negative always implies the positive. The command not to take God's name in vain indicates a command to "serve God acceptably with reverence and godly fear: for our God is a consuming fire." Hebrews 12:28, 29. Those who fulfill this command will approach the Eternal with a reverent attitude, recognizing the holy character of His name. Reverence is the very gateway to the divine presence. Since God's holiness is in His name, the humble suppliant will begin his worship with the reverent declaration, "Hallowed be Thy name."

Who is "the LORD thy God," that we should reverence His name? This is virtually the question Pharaoh asked Moses when he spoke to him in the name of "the LORD God of Israel," and asked him to release Israel from bondage: "Pharaoh said, Who is the LORD, that I should obey His voice to let Israel go? I know not the LORD, neither will I let Israel go." Exodus 5:1, 2. It was because the king of Egypt did not know the Lord that he refused to respect and obey Him. This is always true. His name is taken in vain only by those who really do not know Him. If they knew Him they would love Him and reverence His holy name.

"Everything that is comes from Him. If you speak of power, His is the greatest conceivable. If you speak of wisdom, His transcends the loftiest comprehension of man. If you think of truth, He is the ultimate reality upon which all else depends. If you think of beauty, He is the author of all that is lovely. If you think of goodness, His character is the ultimate standard. All that we have, and all that we are, we owe to Him. We are dependent upon Him for our very lives; we cannot exist apart from Him. If, therefore, we are in the slightest degree intelligent, if in our hearts there is the least spark of gratitude, if in our souls there is any appreciation of what is fine and true and right, this intelligence and appreciation and gratitude must express themselves in reverence for God."
–JOHN H. POWELL, *The Ten Commandments*, pp. 29, 30.

REVELATION OF CHARACTER

Name and character are inseparable. When we think or speak of a person having a good name, we mean a good character or reputation. *"A good name is rather to be chosen than great riches,"* is a Scriptural expression. God's name sets forth all that He is. On one occasion Moses said to the Lord, *"I beseech Thee, show me Thy glory. And He said, I will make all My goodness pass before thee, and I will proclaim the name of the LORD before thee; and will be gracious to whom I will be gracious, and will show mercy on whom I will show mercy." "And the LORD descended in the cloud, and stood with him there, and proclaimed the name of the LORD. And the LORD passed by before him, and proclaimed, The LORD, The LORD God, merciful and gracious, long-suffering, and abundant in goodness and truth, keeping mercy for thousands, forgiving iniquity and transgression and sin, and that will by no means clear the guilty; visiting the iniquity of the fathers upon the children, and upon the children's children, unto the third and to the fourth generation. And Moses made haste, and bowed his head toward the earth, and worshiped."* Exodus 33:18, 19; 34:5-8.

In proclaiming His character to Moses, the Lord proclaimed His name. This revelation placed Moses in the proper attitude of reverence for worship. At the time when the decalogue was given, all names were significant. A child was named in memory of some event connected with his birth, or as a prayer or prophecy of what

57

the parents desired him to be. The name was the revelation of a character. The name of God is equivalent to God Himself. To call upon His name is to call upon Him. His name sums up all that He has revealed Himself to be. Just as we do not separate a person from the name he bears, so God and His name are inseparable. In the incarnation of Christ, *"God was manifest in the flesh."* The Son of God came to reveal God to man; to make known His character. In His prayer to the Father, Jesus said, *"I have manifested Thy name unto the men Thou gavest Me out of the world."* John 17:6.

A REVEREND NAME

"Reverend" is used but once in the Scriptures, and then it is applied to the name of God. *"Holy and reverend is His name."* Psalms 111:9. Since *"reverend"* is one of the titles of God, it should never be attached to the name of a man. The character of God is so great that there are no less than 250 names, titles, and emblems used in the Scriptures to describe Him and His work. They are all summed up in the statement, *"His name shall be called Wonderful."* All His names are holy and reverend. While the sum of God's names constitutes a revelation of His divine nature, no one name or all of them combined can fully exhaust the unsearchable riches of His matchless character.

The name Jehovah was considered so sacred among the Jews that they refused to pronounce it. At one time they refused to step on a piece of paper lying on the ground for fear the name of God might be written on it. This is doubtless an extreme position but modern Christians are in great danger of going to the other extreme, and by too often and carelessly using the name of God they drag it down to the level of the common and profane. We too often forget that when we take the name of God upon our lips we are on holy ground. God's name is used too often in our praying and speaking, so that it becomes altogether too common. In the model prayer His name is mentioned but once, and then it is *"Our Father."* And yet many today use the name of God twenty and thirty times in a single prayer. Even the heathen believed that they polluted the names of their deities by using them too often.

PROFANITY

While the prohibition of profanity of speech, or cursing, is not the primary object of the third commandment, it is nevertheless included. What we speak of as common swearing has been called "the most gratuitous of all sins" because it is "not only sinful, but useless." It is silly, vulgar, and profane. The word "profane" is composed of two Latin words, *pro*, meaning "in front of," and *fane*, meaning "the temple." It indicates irreverence for holy things. It is defying God, as it were, in the very vicinity of His holy temple. It is trampling reverence, the queen of virtues, underfoot. The door of God's holy temple, representing His presence, is closed in the face of the profane.

Profanity is never a sign of intelligence. It is always most prevalent among the crude, uncultured, and illiterate. If it is intended as humor, it is humor of a very low order. It is more often mere bluff as a substitute for courage. If there is a God, profaning His name is highly dangerous. If there is no God it is useless and worse than vanity, a sign of crass ignorance. Would anyone be so debased and irreverent as to profane the name of his mother, sister, wife, or sweetheart? Would he not defend the honor of any loved one thus infamously treated? What then should be our attitude toward the name of One who is as high above us as the heavens are higher than the earth, One who is infinitely pure and holy?

A man thus excused his weakness to his minister: *"I have such an awful temper, but I sort of excuse myself because I got it from my father. He had an awful temper, and I am just like him."* The minister wisely answered, *"Well, were you born again?"* *"Yes,"* was the answer. *"Were you born of God?"* *"Yes,"* was the reply. *"Is God your Father?"* Again the answer was in the affirmative. The minister drove the lesson home with the question, *"What kind of temper did you get when you were born again?"* Those who experience the new birth inherit a new disposition.

The genuine Christian will avoid the use of even those bywords which verge on profanity, especially the words which are attributes of God's character, such as "goodness," "gracious," and "mercy." He will also refrain from saying "Gee," which is an abbreviation for "Jesus." It is said that the Japanese language is the only one in the world with no profane words of any kind in it. It is therefore impossible to swear in pure Japanese. This should also be true of the

Christian language. The divine promise is, *"Then will I turn to the people a pure language, that they may all call upon the name of the LORD, to serve Him with one consent." "The remnant of Israel shall not do iniquity, nor speak lies; neither shall a deceitful tongue be found in their mouth: for they shall feed and lie down, and none shall make them afraid."* Zephaniah 3: 9, 13.

FALSE SWEARING

False swearing is also forbidden in the third commandment. *"Ye shall not swear by My name falsely, neither shalt thou profane the name of thy God."* Leviticus 19:12. This does not forbid the taking of a judicial oath in the name of the Lord, for this the Lord commanded His people to do: *"Thou shalt fear the LORD thy God, and serve Him, and shalt swear by His name."* Deuteronomy 6:13. Since God confirms His own word by swearing by Himself, and the angels affirm the truthfulness of their messages by a solemn appeal to the character of the Creator, surely it is proper for Christians to take the judicial oath as a confirmation of the truthfulness of their testimony. (See **Isaiah 45: 23; Hebrews 6:13; Revelation 10: 5-7.**) The angel of the latter text is really symbolic of a heaven-sent message heralded to the world by God's people.

The intent of the third commandment is that God's name is never to be linked with falsehood by the violation of a solemn oath or vow. It is not swearing, but false swearing that is forbidden. The command means that we cannot take an oath in God's name and then lie on that assurance. A Christian's word ought to be as good as his oath. No finer compliment was ever paid than that given the Baptists of Holland by **William, Prince of Orange**, king of the Dutch Republic, when he said, *"Their yea was equal to their oath."*

Perjury is one of the greatest crimes of the modern world. It is almost universal. God's name is presumptuously and blasphemously taken in vain by those who take the judicial oath to *"tell the truth, the whole truth, and nothing but the truth, so help me God,"* and then bear false witness. This is an insult to God who is the truth, and the author of all truth. It is treating His name with contempt and defying His holy law. The Lord declares that He will not hold such "guiltless" in the final day of reckoning. The person who takes the judicial oath should realize that he is bearing testimony not alone before a human court but also before the Judge

60

of the universe. If he bears false testimony he is lying to God as well as to man.

WARNING OF CHRIST

In His sermon on the mount Jesus sounded a solemn warning: *"Ye have heard that it hath been said by them of old time, Thou shalt not forswear thyself, but shalt perform unto the Lord thine oaths: but I say unto you, Swear not at all; neither by heaven; for it is God's throne: nor by the earth; for it is His footstool: neither by Jerusalem; for it is the city of the great King. Neither shalt thou swear by thy head, because thou canst not make one hair white or black. But let your communication be, Yea, yea; Nay, nay: for whatsoever is more than these cometh of evil."* Matthew 5: 33-37.

But this cannot be interpreted as forbidding the judicial oath, because Jesus Himself bore testimony under judicial oath before the supreme tribunal of the Hebrews. When the high priest said to Him, *"I adjure Thee by the living God, that Thou tell us whether Thou be the Christ, the Son of God,"* Jesus answered, *"Thou hast said,"* which is equivalent to saying *"I am."* (See **Matthew 26: 63, 64.**) In His previous statement Jesus was condemning as useless, oaths used in ordinary conversation. The Jews at that time had carried this practice to great extremes, using solemn oaths to confirm almost every statement.

On the other hand the Jews did not always require an oath in their courts because of the statement in the Talmud that "whosoever will not tell the truth without an oath, would not scruple to assert falsehood with an oath." Here a great truth is stated. So trifling and useless has become the use of the judicial oath in our modern courts, because of the frequency of perjury, that some judges have suggested that it be dispensed with. It does not seem to curb the lying tendency in the least degree. Wordsworth set forth this popular feeling when he wrote:

"Earth is sick
And Heaven is weary of the hollow words
Which states and kingdoms utter when they talk
Of truth and justice."

61

Under Hebrew law false witnesses were dealt with very severely.

"Hebrew law provided that false witnesses should suffer the penalty provided for the commission of the crime which they sought by their testimony to fix upon the accused."
                                    –WALTER M. CHANDLER,
                                    The Trial of Jesus, Vol. I, p.140.

This rule was based on the divine instruction given in **Deuteronomy 19:18-20:** *"The judges shall make diligent inquisition: and, behold, if the witness be a false witness, and hath testified falsely against his brother; then shall ye do unto him, as he had thought to have done unto his brother: so shalt thou put the evil away from among you. And those which remain shall hear, and fear, and shall henceforth commit no more any such evil among you."*

The genuine Christian does not need an oath in order to tell the truth. With him yea and nay, or yes and no, should be sufficient. Those who must be put under solemn oath in order to get them to tell the truth will not hesitate to lie after they have sworn to testify truthfully. Lying is one of the worst of all the character-destroying and soul-polluting sins of this generation. It deals the deadliest blow against the liar himself. He always hurts himself more than the person lied about. *"Sin has many tools, but a lie is the handle which fits them all,"* is an ancient proverb. Two of the ten commandments deal with the sin of falsehood, the third and the ninth. This indicates how hateful lying is to the Lord. In the third commandment the Lord protects His own name, and in the ninth our names are safeguarded.

IRREVERENCE FOR GOD'S WORD

The sin of taking God's name in vain includes irreverence for His Word. *"Thou hast magnified Thy word above all Thy name,"* declared the psalmist in **Psalms 138:2.** The Lord often declared that His name was in His law and His temple. *"My name is there,"* He said. The purpose of the Scriptures and the plan of salvation is to reveal the name or character of God to man. We therefore profane His name when we show irreverence for His Word. All jesting and joking based on Scriptural statements is a dangerous species of profanity. It is very easy to create a laugh in a modern audience by frivolous association of that which is grotesque with the Word of

God. The Bible should never be used as material for manufacturing jests. Preaching is altogether too serious and solemn a matter to be mixed with the unholy fire of the comical and ludicrous. Inattention, whispering, laughing, and all forms of disrespectful behavior during public worship are a form of profanity and are forbidden in the third commandment. In fact, it is blasphemy that will not go unpunished in the judgment.

The following instruction should be carefully heeded by every worshiper of Jehovah: *"Keep thy foot when thou goest to the house of God, and be more ready to hear, than to give the sacrifice of fools: for they consider not that they do evil. Be not rash with thy mouth, and let not thine heart be hasty to utter anything before God: for God is in heaven, and thou upon earth: therefore let thy words be few."* Ecclesiastes 5:1, 2. Worshipers who do not show respect for God's house or listen to His Word offer the sacrifice of fools instead of saints.

THE SIN OF HYPOCRISY

Perhaps the chief application of the third commandment is to the sin of hypocrisy. We play the hypocrite when we lie with our lives. Originally the term *"hypocrite"* was applied to an actor-one who pretended to be what he was not for the purpose of entertaining. It is now applied to those who play a double role in their daily conduct, professing to one thing and acting the part of another. No other sin so aroused the indignation of Christ as that of hypocrisy, and against it He hurled His most terrible woes.

The third commandment is against lying in all forms, whether it be lying with our lips, or lying with our lives. Hypocrisy is the worst of all the forms of lying or bearing false witness. The person who accepts Christ and becomes a Christian takes the name of Christ. The Lord speaks of *"My people, which are called by My name."* 2 Chronicles 7:14. *"We are called by Thy name; leave us not,"* cried one of the prophets. (Jeremiah 14:9.) The person who professes to be a Christian and at the same time lives a life that is a denial of his profession, is taking God's name in vain. A false professor of Christianity is a blasphemer. God's name is taken in vain by a profession without the possession of holiness; by saying, *"Lord, Lord,"* with the lips and then denying Him by the conduct.

63

This sort of false swearing is described in **Isaiah 48:1, 2**: *"Hear ye this, O house of Jacob, which are called by the name of Israel, and are come forth out of the waters of Judah, which swear by the name of the LORD, and make mention of the God of Israel, but not in truth, nor in righteousness. For they call themselves of the holy city, and stay themselves upon the God of Israel; the LORD of hosts is His name."* It is proper to swear by the name of the Lord, but it must be done in truth and righteousness. To make use of any one of God's names while not living in harmony with its revelation of His character is taking it in vain.

VAIN WORSHIP

Jesus warned against vain worship, or the taking of God's name in vain. He said: *"Not everyone that saith unto Me, Lord, Lord, shall enter into the kingdom of heaven; but he that doeth the will of My Father which is in heaven. Many will say to Me in that day, Lord, Lord, have we not prophesied in Thy name? and in Thy name have cast out devils? and in Thy name done many wonderful works? And then will I profess unto them, I never knew you: depart from Me, ye that work iniquity."* Matthew 7:21-23.

On one other occasion Jesus rebuked the Jews for making the commandments of God of none effect by their tradition and then said: *"Ye hypocrites, well did Esaias prophesy of you, saying, This people draweth nigh unto Me with their mouth, and honoreth Me with their lips; but their heart is far from Me. But in vain they do worship Me, teaching for doctrines the commandments of men."* Matthew 15:7-9. There is a great deal of this vain worship in the modern religious world, even in Christendom. Jesus said, *"Why call ye Me, Lord, Lord, and do not the things which I say?"* Luke 6:46.

It is positively dangerous to use the name. of the Lord when we do not know Him or are not known by Him. Many professed Christians feel secure, as far as the third commandment is concerned, because they do not use vile oaths or vulgar language, and would be shocked if they were told that they are as guilty as if they did. A vulgar oath may never have stained their lips, but they are breaking the third commandment every day and hour by hypocritical lives.

God's name can be hallowed only by doing His Will on earth as it is done in heaven, which is the evidence Of heavenly citizenship. Those who are called by God's name are under the most solemn obligation to conduct themselves in a manner worthy of that name. This is possible only with those who have experienced the new birth and the imputed and imparted righteousness of Christ. When the heart and motives are pure, the worship will be acceptable to God. **John Ruskin**, in his book *Modern Painters,* declared that *"a bad man cannot paint a good picture."* The opposite is also true. Vain worship is the result of a vain life. A farmer was being shown some modernistic paintings which he was unable to appreciate. *"You see,"* said the guide, *"the paintings depict not the mere things the artist saw, but his state of mind."* The farmer retorted, *"If I had a mind that looked like that I'd never expose it!"* But we always expose our state of mind in the things we do. Often what we do makes so much noise that others cannot hear what we say. The third commandment condemns such hypocrisy and vain worship.

THREATENED JUDGMENT

"The Lord will not hold him guiltless that taketh His name in vain," is equivalent to saying that the Lord will pronounce him guilty. This is one of the two commands in the decalogue that has a threat attached to it. *"Guiltless"* in the Hebrew means *"clean,"* indicating that a person's attitude toward God's name is the test of his moral cleanness, or of the state of his character. Many are inclined to look upon profanity in its various forms as a trivial matter, but this awful threatening should convince them that the Lord considers vain worship as one of the worst of sins, one that will not go unpunished.

THE DAY OF WORSHIP

6

"**R**emember the Sabbath day, to keep it holy. Six days shalt thou labor, and do all thy work: but the seventh day is the Sabbath of the LORD thy God: in it thou shalt not do any work, thou, nor thy son, nor thy daughter, thy manservant, nor thy maidservant, nor thy cattle, nor thy stranger that is within thy gates: for in six days the LORD made heaven and earth, the sea, and all that in them is, and rested the seventh day: wherefore the LORD blessed the Sabbath day, and hallowed it." Exodus 20: 8-11. (See also **Deuteronomy 5:12-15.**)

The fourth commandment closes the first section of the decalogue, which sets forth man's obligations to his Creator. The four commands of the first table of the law are arranged in their logical order. The first proclaims the true object of worship and warns against false gods. The second sets forth the true mode of worship and prohibits false forms of religion. The third gives the proper approach for worship and warns against profanity, irreverence, and hypocrisy. The fourth designates the special time for worship by consecrating the seventh day of each week as the memorial of creation and of deliverance from the bondage of sin.

After proclaiming Himself as the creator and urging His claim upon His creatures, God provides for specified periods of worship, in order to maintain the proper relationship between man and his Maker. At regular times man must turn from all his secular pursuits to spiritual things. He must be made to realize that all of his time and activities are planned and ordered of God and that his physical and spiritual life depend upon each other and must therefore both be properly nourished. The divine command to worship the Creator implies the absolute necessity for the setting apart of a special time to worship Him.

The Sabbath commandment is the climax of the first table of the decalogue and therefore of all relationships between the human and the divine. The Sabbath is the meeting place of God and man. As the weekly appointment for communion and worship, the Sabbath brings heaven and earth together. It has been appropriately called the Christian's Ascension Day, because on that day he is translated from the temporal into the spiritual realm; he ascends into the atmosphere of heaven. The Sabbath brings heaven to earth and is a reminder of the Paradise home that was lost through sin. It is also a pledge of the Paradise to be restored through Christ.

The Sabbath is the most ancient of all religious institutions. It had its origin in Paradise before the fall and will continue through all eternity in the redeemed state. *"As the new heavens and the new earth, which I will make, shall remain before Me, saith the LORD, so shall your seed and your name remain. And it shall come to pass, that from one new moon to another, and from one Sabbath to another, shall all flesh come to worship before Me, saith the LORD."* Isaiah 66: 22, 23.

The fourth is the first positive command of the decalogue and the only one in the first table. The fifth commandment is the only other positive requirement, and that has to do with the home. It is a significant fact that the Sabbath and the home are safeguarded in the very bosom of the law. They are the first two of all divine institutions, having both originated in Paradise before the fall of man. They constitute the foundations of religion and society, and they will both continue in the Paradise restored.

D. L. Moody said:

"I believe that the Sabbath question today is a vital one for the whole country. It is the burning question of the present time. If you give up the Sabbath the church goes; if you give up the church the home goes; and if the home goes the nation goes. That is the direction in which we are traveling."

–Weighed and Wanting, p. 47.

A TWOFOLD COMMAND

The fourth commandment does not deal with the Sabbath alone. It embraces the entire week and includes the six working days as well as the Sabbath of rest. This is because labor and rest are closely related. The Sabbath gets a part of its significance from the six days of activity. A person does not need to rest till after he has labored. The Sabbath should therefore always follow the days of labor rather than precede them. The seventh day rather than the first is the logical time for rest. Observing the first day of the week as the Sabbath is a reversal of the divine order.

The command to work precedes the command to rest, because those who do not labor are unprepared to rest and worship. On the other hand those who refuse to stop for periods of rest are never able to render the best service in labor. The person who properly observes the first table of the decalogue must be a worker as well as a worshiper. Careful investigation has proved that man can accomplish more work in a given period when he rests one day in every seven.

The command to rest at stated intervals included the earth itself. The Lord said to Moses: *"Speak unto the children of Israel, and say unto them, When ye come into the land which I give you, then shall the land keep a sabbath unto the LORD.... In the seventh year shall be a sabbath of rest unto the land, a sabbath unto the LORD."* Leviticus 25: 2-4. This also is now known to be necessary to the best interest of the soil. All the commands of God are based on both reason and necessity.

The need to labor is just as fundamental, universal, and imperative as the need to rest. The command, *"Six days shalt thou labor, and do all thy work,"* or *"all your business"* (Moffatt), is just as binding as the command to keep holy the Sabbath day. The need to labor was not the result of the fall, although the curse increased its necessity. Labor was a part of the original plan, and before man sinned he was put to work taking care of the Garden of Eden. *"The LORD God took the man, and put him into the Garden of Eden to dress it and to keep it."* Genesis 2:15.

The Creator filled the earth with everything needed to sustain physical life, but man must labor to produce and gather it. Labor is not a curse. It is one of the greatest blessings of life. It is really a sin to be willingly idle, and indolent people can never get the full enjoyment out of the Sabbath. The command to labor is often repeated in the New Testament: *"We beseech you, brethren, that ye... do your own business, and to work with your own hands, as we commanded you; that ye may walk honestly toward them that are without, and that ye may have lack of nothing."* 1 Thessalonians 4:10-12. *"When we were with you, this we commanded you, that if any would not work, neither should he eat."* 2 Thessalonians 3:10. This is the same principle laid down in the fourth commandment of the law that proclaims *"the whole duty of man."* We must work during the six working days, or the Sabbath loses much of its significance.

A THREEFOLD NATURE

Man was created with a threefold nature, and the physical, mental, and spiritual must be kept properly balanced and nourished if man is to meet the ideal of the Creator. The fourth commandment sets forth the proper balance between the physical, mental, and spiritual. **Talmage** declared, *"Our bodies are seven-day clocks and need to be wound up, and if they are not wound up they run down into the grave. No man can continually break the Sabbath and keep his physical and mental health."*

It has often been demonstrated that six days of labor and one day of rest is the proper balance from a physical and mental viewpoint, and it is therefore dangerous to run counter to the divine plan. This phase of the subject is beautifully set forth by **G. Campbell Morgan:**

> *"Thus the Sabbath had its ethical meaning. From the quiet calm of the Sabbath day man returned to the necessary and swift movements of the six. As he did so, the integrity and justice of the things with which he had communed in the hours of rest, touched and influenced him in all the hours of work. He delved deeply, and measured justly, and weighed righteously for six days, because on the seventh he became conscious of the balances of the sanctuary and the righteousness of God. Thus the two commandments are one, so interrelated that they can never be separated. To fail in obedience to the one is to make it impossible to obey the other. Obedience to each creates the power to obey*

the other. Work makes worship and worship fits for work....

"Not only the law of God, tender and beneficent, but the law of human society, too often stern and cruel, says to man, Thou shalt work! The fact that there are any who escape obedience to the command is the saddest fact of sociology. If the necessity for work were still understood in all its divine bearings, no human being... would be allowed to eat a meal until that meal had been purchased by the contribution of a quota of toil to the commonwealth of work."

–The Ten Commandments, pp. 47-49.

Fortunately almost the entire human race is compelled to obey this first part of the fourth commandment, not willingly, but of necessity. It is a question of life and death, or at least it was before the welfare system was introduced. This human regulation is contrary to the divine plan.

The word *"Sabbath"* means *"rest,"* not only physical, but spiritual. In its primitive pre-Semitic name *"sabbath"* meant *"soul rest."* The fourth is the only command of the decalogue that begins with the word *"remember."* This indicates first of all that the Sabbath had been previously instituted and was known to man. It was not a new institution. In the commandment itself is the evidence that it had been instituted at creation, and the example of the Creator at the close of creation week is given as the reason why man should observe it. There can be no other possible reason for the Lord's spending six days in the work of creation except as an example for man to imitate. He could have created all things in one day, or even in one hour, and He did not need any rest Himself, for *"the everlasting God... fainteth not, neither is weary."* **Isaiah 40: 28.**

Since *"the Sabbath was made for man, and not man for the Sabbath"* (**Mark 2: 27**), the Sabbath must have been made and given to men when man was made, and the blessing and hallowing of the day must have been for man's benefit. It set the day apart for a holy use and made its observance a special blessing and privilege.

The existence of the week between creation and Sinai indicates the existence and observance of the Sabbath, for the Sabbath and the week are inseparable. Cain and Abel brought their sacrifices to the gate of Paradise *"in the end of days,"* which doubtless refers to the only period into which the days were measured, the days of the week. (See **Genesis 4:3, 4:5**)

"The repeated mention of seven days seems an intimation of the observance of Sabbath in the ark; after the ordinances of which, the dove was sent out."–**Scott's Bible**. The sixteenth chapter of **Exodus** shows clearly that the Sabbath was observed before the giving of the law.

THE UNIVERSAL SABBATH

Since the reason for the Sabbath is based on the law of man's very nature, and its observance enforced by God's example at creation and command at Sinai, it cannot be a racial or dispensational institution. As a universal institution observed as the memorial of creation in all Bible times and destined to continue through all eternity, the Sabbath is a part of God's eternal purpose. That the advent of Christ and the gospel dispensation did not altar the Sabbath is evident from the fact that it was strictly observed by Christ and His apostles and the early Christians for several centuries before a change was gradually effected. We are also told that *"there remaineth therefore a rest* ["keeping of a Sabbath," margin] *to the people of God,"* and that only can remain which had previously existed. The same scripture says that *"he that is entered into His rest"* must cease *"from his own works."* (**Hebrews 4: 4-10**.) Modern Christians are asked to follow the example of the Creator at creation and thus live in harmony with the fourth commandment.

The need of worship is just as universal as the need of labor and rest, and since true religion cannot exist without the Sabbath, the fourth commandment cannot be local, temporal, or ceremonial. It is a perpetual and universal institution.

D. L. Moody said:

"I honestly believe that this commandment is just as binding today as it ever was. I have talked with men who have said that it has been abrogated, but they have never been able to point to any place in the Bible where God repealed it. When Christ was on earth, He did nothing to set it aside; He freed it from the traces under which the scribes and Pharisees had put it, and gave it its true place.... It is just as practicable and as necessary

71

for men today as it ever was-in fact, more than ever, because we live in such an intense age. The Sabbath was binding in Eden, and it has been in force ever since. This fourth commandment begins with the word 'remember,' showing that the Sabbath already existed when God wrote this law on the tables of stone at Sinai. How can men claim that this one commandment has been done away with when they will admit that the other nine are still binding?"

—Weighed and Wanting, pp. 46, 47.

If the Sabbath had been intended as a temporary institution for the Jews alone, it would not have been placed in the very bosom of the moral law that is acknowledged by practically all denominations to be eternal and unchangeable. It cannot be extracted from the heart of the decalogue, where Jehovah wrote it with His own finger in imperishable granite.

"You cannot interfere with the fabric of the moral law by removing one of its integral parts, without endangering the fabric of the whole. You cannot disobey one commandment of the moral law and remain moral."
—JOHN BURR, *Studies on the Ten Commandments,* p. 71.

LEST WE FORGET

"Remember the Sabbath day, to keep it holy," indicates the danger of forgetfulness as far as the Sabbath is concerned. Human memory is treacherous and undependable. Every day we are reminded of our proneness to forget. It is always easier to forget a duty than a prohibition. The command to do what is right is more difficult to remember than the command not to do what is wrong. The very temptation to do evil acts as a reminder of the prohibition, so that we are not permitted to forget.

It seems especially easy to forget the Sabbath and its divine purpose in the plan of redemption. Because of its great importance in the sustaining of spiritual life, the enemy of all righteousness has made every effort to cause men to forget its significance and sacredness. The tendency has always been to bring the Sabbath down to the level of the common or profane days of the week. Said the prophet concerning God's ancient people to whom the law was first given: *"Her priests have violated My law, and have profaned Mine holy things: they have put no difference between the holy and profane, neither have they showed difference between the unclean and the clean, and have hid their eyes from My Sabbaths, and I am profaned among them."* Ezekiel 22: 26.

Because the Sabbath has been divinely blessed and sanctified, it is different from any other day of the week. Only God can make anything or anybody holy, and only a day sanctified by the Lord can be kept sacredly, and then only by a holy people.

DAY OF WORSHIP

We must not forget that the Sabbath is first of all a day of worship. The need for worship is just as universal as the need for rest. Those who forget to rest soon forget to worship, and the reverse is also true. Christ is our example in all things including Sabbathkeeping. A part of His Sabbathkeeping was attendance at public worship. In **Luke 4:16** we are told that it was His *"custom"* to go to the synagogue on the Sabbath day. This was also the fixed custom of Paul and the other apostles. (See **Acts 16:13; 17:2; 18: 4,11.**)

True Sabbathkeeping includes *"an holy convocation,"* or assembly or calling together, during its sacred hours, and this must not be neglected. (**Leviticus 23:3; Hebrews 10:25,26.**) The shewbread, or the *"bread of the presence,"* was placed fresh on the table every Sabbath morning. A new and fresh supply of the bread of life is spread on the spiritual banquet table at the Sabbath morning service, and those who neglect to partake of this feast do so at the peril of their souls, for spiritual food is necessary if spiritual health and strength are to be maintained. To this spiritual festival all are graciously invited, but many *"with one consent"* begin *"to make excuse,"* and what flimsy excuses most of them are! What a reformation would be wrought if modern Christians were as punctual and enthusiastic about meeting their appointment with God as in attending a social gathering or meeting a business appointment.

The Sabbath was never intended as a day for sleep and inactivity. Sabbath resting is not loafing. It is not a day for indolence on the one hand, or for selfish pleasure and indulgence on the other.

73

It is a holyday rather than a holiday. The six days are for secular work; the seventh is to be devoted to worship and spiritual service. Religious activity is to characterize the seventh day. It should never be a day of gloom, but one of sacred joy. It is to be called *"a delight."* It should be a time of spiritual refreshing when the river of life, as it were, overflows its banks and brings to our thirsty souls the blessings of life and growth and fruitfulness.

Jesus declared that *"it is lawful to do well on the Sabbath days,"* and He demonstrated what He meant by works of charity and necessity. Someone has said that *"good deeds have no Sabbath."* Ministry to the sick and the relief of suffering, as well as all other forms of missionary work of the unselfish and non-remunerative variety, are a part of good Sabbathkeeping. Whenever possible a part of the day should be spent amid the scenes of nature, because the Sabbath is the memorial of creation. Contemplation of God's creative works is proper and profitable Sabbath observance, provided we have first attended a convocation of God's people in His house of worship. **Moody** declared that *"the number of church services attended ought to be measured by the person's ability to enjoy them and get good from them, without being wearied."* This is good counsel. It is possible to have too many services on the Sabbath, so that the day becomes a burden rather than a delight.

THINGS FORBIDDEN

Many things that are perfectly proper on other days must not be permitted to pollute the Sabbath. The divine counsel and promise is: *"If thou turn away thy foot from the Sabbath, from doing thy pleasure on My holy day; and call the Sabbath a delight, the holy of the LORD, honorable; and shalt honor Him, not doing thine own ways, nor finding thine own pleasure, nor speaking thine own words: then shalt thou delight thyself in the LORD; and I will cause thee to ride upon the high places of the earth, and feed thee with the heritage of Jacob thy father: for the mouth of the LORD hath spoken it."* Isaiah 58:13, 14.

The foot is the symbol of travel just as the hand is the symbol of labor. The Sabbath is trampled underfoot when we travel for business or mere pleasure on that day. The Jews were forbidden to travel farther than the synagogue or temple on the Sabbath. Travel to divine services or on charitable or missionary ventures is proper on the Sabbath. But neither our feet nor cars should be permitted to go our *"own ways"* or to find our *"own pleasure"* on God's holy day. Nor should we speak our *"own words"* by planning work for the coming week or discussing business or personal affairs. All secular matters should be forgotten on the Sabbath.

In commenting on this Scripture, **Bishop Andrews** said: *"To keep the Sabbath in an idle manner is the Sabbath of the oxen and asses; to pass it in a jovial manner is the Sabbath of the golden calf, when the people sat down to eat and drink, and rose up to play; to keep it in a surfeiting and wantonness is the Sabbath of Satan, the devil's holiday."*

Secular reading and radio and television programs should all be eliminated on the sacred hours of the Sabbath. The edges of the Sabbath should be sacredly guarded from being trespassed upon, for one minute of the day divinely blessed and sanctified is just as sacred as another. There should be just as much of a distinction between the Sabbath and the other days of the week as there is between a Christian and a worldling.

A NEW CREATION

The Sabbath is a memorial of the new as well as the old creation. It is a sign of creative power whenever and wherever manifested. Redemption or recreation requires the same power as the original creation, and the Sabbath is the memorial of both. Redemption is the restoration of the original creation and all that it contained, which included the Sabbath. In **Isaiah 56:1-7** a blessing is pronounced on all who lay *"hold on"* and keep *"the Sabbath from polluting it"* and keep *"from doing any evil."* The promised blessing includes *"the eunuchs that keep My Sabbaths"* and *"the sons of the stranger, that join themselves to the LORD"* and *"all people."* The Sabbath is therefore the sign of victory over sin, or of redemption from sin.

In **Ezekiel 20:12** the Sabbath is declared to be the sign of sanctification, or holiness. Sanctified people will observe the sanctified day. The Sabbath is the sign and memorial of the new birth, the evidence of the work of the Creator in remaking or restoring that which was lost through sin. It is the outward evidence that the image or character of God has been or is being restored in the soul. At the close of creation week the Lord proclaimed His

75

work finished and then rested on the seventh day. At the close of His work of redemption the Lord cried out, *"It is finished,"* and again rested on the Sabbath. The Sabbath is therefore an appropriate memorial of both creations. It is the Sabbath of twice-born men and women, of those who have experienced both creations. To others it can have no special significance. It is the Lord's day, the Christian Sabbath, the day on which sin-pardoned men and women enter into God's Eden rest by ceasing from their *"own works, as God did from His."* Hebrews 4:10. *"There remaineth therefore a Sabbath rest for the people of God."* Verse 9, R. V.

THE FAMILY GOVERNMENT

7

"**H** *onor thy father and thy mother: that thy days may be long upon the land which the* LORD *thy God giveth thee.*" **Exodus 20:12.**

The first table of the decalogue deals with man's relations with and obligations to his Creator. The first four commandments tell man how and when to worship, and warn against irreverence and impiety in word and conduct. The second table deals with human relationships. These six commandments tell us how to treat one another, and it is therefore appropriate that the regulations of human relations should begin with the family life in the home, the place where society has its origin.

The family is the most important and fundamental unit in society and government. Respect for parental authority and obedience to parental law are the foundation of all order and organization. As goes the home, so goes society, the nation, and the world. The fifth commandment is properly placed at the beginning of the second table, its position thus indicating a divine arrangement. Family relationships constitute the beginning of all human relationships, which are set forth in the second division of the law and have been appropriately called "the six pillars which uphold the social order of the world." Since the fifth commandment deals with obedience to all lawful authority in that formative period of life when characters are molded and destinies are determined, how true is the saying that "the hand that rocks the cradle rules the world."

Because in so many ways the parents stand in the place of God to their children until they arrive at the age of discretion and accountability, the fifth commandment is closely related to the first four. It has been spoken of as the bridge that connects the two tables of the law. During the earlier years the parent is to the child what God is to the adult-the lawgiver, the overseer, and the provider. The fact that the attitude of the child toward the parent determines his attitude toward God in later years gives the fifth commandment a double significance. When the home life is what it should be, the children are almost certain to fulfill both tables of the law and respect both divine and human authority.

Since true morality is impossible without true religion, proper human relations have their root in the relations that should exist between the human and the divine, as set forth in the first table. The foundations of both religion and morality are laid in the home, and therefore the fifth commandment occupies a significant place in the bosom of the decalogue. The close relationship between the fourth and fifth commandments is indicated by **Leviticus 19:3**: *"Ye shall fear every man his mother, and his father, and keep My Sabbaths: I am the LORD your God."* Reverence for the Sabbath must begin in the home, where respect for divine and human law has its origin.

Another evidence of the importance of this commandment is the fact that parenthood is copartnership with God in the work of creation. Reproduction is a form of creation. What greater honor could God bestow upon human beings than to share with them the power to perpetuate His creative works? This realization of the holy functions of parenthood will place marriage on a moral elevation seldom recognized in this world of sin. It will give a sacredness to family relationships that will ennoble and dignify the marriage institution, which is being trampled into the dust.

THE LAW OF GOD

While the decalogue is divided into two tables and ten commands, it is one law-the law of God. Even though the second table deals with human relations, its commands are nevertheless the commands of God, the violation of which is sin, and the wages of which is death. Sin against man is primarily sin against God. While the first table is the foundation of the second, both are part of the same structure. The same God who said, *"Thou shalt love the LORD thy God"* and *"Him only shalt thou serve,"* also said, *"Thou shalt love thy neighbor as thyself."* It is impossible to properly love and serve one another until we first learn to love and obey God. The true relationship between parents and their children is based on the relationship between God and the human family.

Children should therefore honor their parents, who symbolize God to them during the earlier years of life. They owe their very existence to their parents, are made in their image, inherit their characteristics, and depend on them for the things that sustain life. How could there be, therefore, a more binding obligation of honor than that which children owe their parents? It is so primary and fundamental that the attitude toward all other commands of the decalogue is affected by it. Obedience to parental law directly affects every other relationship in life.

FAMILY GOVERNMENT

Paul declared that *"the powers that be are ordained of God,"* and this applies to family as well as national government. The family is a divine institution, having been established by God Himself in the Garden of Eden before the entrance of sin. With the first family, human society had its beginning. As His representatives, parents are clothed with divine authority to rule the family government. Rebellion against parental authority is therefore rebellion against God.

It is true that some parents do not merit the honor and respect of their children, and this is often used as an excuse for disobedience. But this cannot entirely excuse disobedience and neglect. There is a moral obligation that can never be ignored regardless of the circumstances. Let us turn the tables and consider what would happen to the home if parents would fulfill their obligations to their children on the basis of their conduct and character, regardless of blood relationship and its binding claims. Suppose parents loved and cared for their children only if or when they were lovable and angelic in character and disposition, and excused themselves of all parental responsibility when they were naughty, disobedient, and even devilish?

The golden rule applies to both parents and children. Neither are perfect enough to deserve all the respect and attention required by the law of God. To use the character and conduct of unworthy parents as an excuse for refusing to honor them with obedience while recipients of their care, or refusing to see that their wants are supplied in old age, is not only a most cowardly act, but it is also a well-nigh unpardonable sin that will not go unpunished in the judgment.

The obligations of the fifth commandment include the entire life of the children. In fact these obligations can never be entirely liquidated, even after the parents are dead. After the children leave the parental home and establish homes of their own, they are not released from the duty to honor father and mother. The days of obedience may cease, but the days of honor never end. The command includes adult life as well as childhood. It sets forth a mutual obligation: that of parents to their children while they are young and needy, and that of children to their parents when they are old and needy.

The nursing home is no place for parents of living children. The obligation of care rests primarily on the children and not on public charity or the church, society, or government. And it must be evident to all that as long as children remain in the home of their parents, regardless of their age and experience, they are under obligations to them that demand respect for their wishes. They have no right to become too willful and independent as long as they dwell under the roof and accept the favors of their parents. Under these circumstances children should show at least as much consideration for their parents as they would as guests in the home of a friend.

MEANING OF HONOR

Honor involves more than mere obedience. It includes affection, respect, and reverence. It means to hold in high esteem because of a recognition of superiority. While no parents in this world of sin are entirely perfect, they are usually more so than their children, and they therefore deserve the respect and courtesy due to superiors. Parents should be honored by their children first of all because of their greater knowledge and fuller experience. Time and experience are very important factors in the attainment of real knowledge and superiority, and can never be supplanted by even a better school education. Because children have had better educational advantages than their parents does not prove that they know more.

Children who receive a better education due to the efforts and sacrifices of the parents, and then break their hearts by an attitude of superiority and feelings of shame, are of all creatures the most mean and contemptible. Regardless of school advantages, parents learn through the very process of passing time, and deserve respectful attention when they speak.

Unfortunately it has always been the attitude of the oncoming generation to consider itself superior to the old, but we must ever remember that progress is slow and that nearly everything worth while in every age came down from former generations. Wisdom was not born with the present generation, nor will it end with its passing. We always learn from our elders more than we discover for ourselves, and should therefore respectfully and courteously rise up before the hoary head and recognize its *"crown of glory,"* especially if it is on the royal heads of father and mother, the king and queen of the family kingdom.

RESULTS OF HONOR

Obedience to righteous laws always brings a just recompense of reward. Young children who honor their parents by lives of subjection and implicit, willing, and joyful obedience, will be richly rewarded in later life, and so will the parents whose character and conduct demand such respect and obedience from their offspring. While parental honor always takes on a new form after the children reach the years of accountability, when they must make their own decisions, yet the fifth commandment does not even then become less binding. It is a well-recognized fact that whenever obedience is properly rendered by children during early life, honor is always accorded the parents in later years, when they need the love, care, and sympathy of their children.

This is what the author of the Hebrews meant when he said: *"We have had fathers of our flesh which corrected us, and we gave them reverence. . . Now no chastening for the present seemeth to be joyous, but grievous: nevertheless afterward it yieldeth the peaceable fruit of righteousness unto them which are exercised thereby."* Hebrews 12:9-11. Righteousness is the chief reward of children for obedience, and reverence is the chief recompense of parents for discipline. Children who are not controlled and disciplined by their parents while they are young are seldom able to control and discipline themselves when they are grown, and they do not respect

81

their parents in old age. Those who respect parental law usually respect civil and divine law.

The lack of regard for authority-parental, civil, and divine-is the greatest evil of the modern world. Self-government has largely broken down and is disappearing, as is evident from the increase of dictatorships in governments on one hand, and the disappearance of democratic forms of government on the other. The breakdown of discipline in the home is largely responsible for the new forms of autocracy that are cursing modern civilization. It is also the chief cause of the tidal wave of crime and lawlessness that is engulfing the nations.

One writer describes the present situation as follows:

"You let children grow up in homes where there is either no authority, or a purely arbitrary one, and you get a generation of lawless people, who respect no authority outside themselves, and have none within themselves. That is pretty largely what you find in my generation. There was a revolt against the arbitrary harshness of our grandfathers, and, as a result, our generation grew up with little or no discipline. And without discipline it is impossible to live a well-ordered life. But discipline must be imposed."
–JOHN H. POWELL, *The Ten Commandments*, p. 66.

Because some parents go to extremes in severity in discipline, there is a great danger that all discipline will be cast aside and the vicious modern doctrine of "self-expression" adopted as a substitute. *"Let your own happiness be your own law,"* is the teaching of atheistic communion, and is the sure road to anarchy and chaos; yet this is the growing philosophy in modern education.

J. Edgar Hoover, former director of the Federal Bureau of Investigation of the United States Government, said:

"So long as we allow our child guidance to be dominated by sentimental theorists who believe that if a child is chastised it may develop an inhibition which will affect its later self-expression, so long as we fail to recognize that discipline is an essential part of human development, just so long will we have an aimless, directionless milling of the herd which can result only

in mental panic and a thorough disregard for the rights of society.

"It is time for America to resurrect that standard of discipline which did much to give this country its rugged, stalwart honesty of purpose, its determination, its achievements. I refer to that parental discipline and guidance which did so much to create law abiding, successful, and forward looking citizens. Too long has that old-fashioned standard been transformed into the wine card of the cocktail bar; into the sapient belief that an immature mind can be granted utter freedom of action without disastrous results....

"The parent who allows any child to run willy-nilly through life obeying every selfish impulse, following the wild ravings of any agitator who orates from a soap box on the corner, is not only doing a foolish thing, but is doing a manifestly unfair and unkind act to the child. It is not generous for a parent to turn its offspring free from all fetters and allow it to run wild in a world which contains as many jungles of criminality as does ours."
— "Wanted: Discipline and Guidance in the Home,"
The Watchman Magazine, January, 1942.

INCLUDES ALL IN AUTHORITY

While the fifth commandment applies primarily to the honoring of parents by their children, in a broader sense it includes respect for all who are in positions of leadership and authority. Children should respect and honor their teachers because, first, they stand in the place of the parents in the work of training and education, and second, they have superior knowledge and experience. In thought, speech, attitude, and conduct, honor is to be shown to whom honor is due, which includes all who are superiors in position and seniors in age and experience. This includes foster parents, stepparents, grandparents, employers, and officials of both church and state.

In both ancient and modern times rulers in various capacities have been called "fathers." Municipal, county, state, and national governments are but enlargements of the family government. The officials of a city government are often spoken of as "the city fathers." The Jews called their spiritual leaders "fathers," as do the Roman Catholics. The following texts give counsel as to the proper honor to be shown spiritual leaders: *"Let the elders that rule well be counted worthy of double honor, especially they who labor in the Word and doctrine." "Obey them that have rule over you, and submit yourselves: for they watch for your souls, as they that must give account, that they may do it with joy, and not with grief: for that is unprofitable for you."* 1 Timothy 5:17; Hebrews 13:17.

THE PROMISE

Long life and material prosperity and success are promised as the reward of obedience to the fifth commandment. *"Honor thy father and thy mother: that thy days may be long upon the land which the LORD thy God giveth thee,"* is the command with its promised recompense for obedience. Paul declares that it is *"the first commandment with promise."* As repeated by Moses later this command reads, *"Honor thy father and mother, as the LORD thy God hath commanded thee; that thy days may be prolonged, and that it may go well with thee, in the land which the LORD thy God giveth thee."* Deuteronomy 5:16.

This inspired translation of the fifth commandment shows that its promise includes more than long life; namely, peace, prosperity, success, and everything that is considered "well." The apostle Paul gives us another inspired version of the fifth commandment that throws even more light on its scope and purpose: *"Children, obey your parents in the Lord: for that is right. Honor thy father and mother; which is the first commandment with promise; that it may be well with thee, and thou mayest live long on the earth."* Ephesians 6:1-3. The promise must have a threefold application: (1) to the individual in this life, (2) to national life, and (3) to the new earth state when God's people will *"long enjoy the work of their hands."* The redeemed will indeed *"live long upon the earth"*; they shall *"dwell therein forever."* This is the ultimate and complete fulfillment of the promise.

It is also a fact that proper habits of living always lengthen life and increase prosperity and happiness, whether in the experience of the individual or the nation. Obedience to parental, civil, and divine law has always brought a lengthening of days and moral and physical strength to a race or nation. It is the chief reason why the Jewish race is so long-lived. The Jews the world around are noted for the respect and honor shown to parents and old age. On the other hand disobedience and lawlessness always tend to shorten individual and national existence. Sin always leads to weakness, disease, and premature death, whereas nobility of character is crowned with a venerable and honorable old age. It is still true that a *"hoary head is a crown of glory, if it be found in the way of righteousness."* **Proverbs 16:31.** A genuine Christian home is the most noble heritage possible.

OTHER SCRIPTURES

The fifth commandment is enforced by many other scriptures in both the Old and New Testaments. Through Moses the Lord said, *"Ye shall fear every man his mother, and his father."* **Leviticus 19:3.** When we consider the time when the decalogue was given and the then prevailing attitude toward womanhood, it is significant that the mother is mentioned along with the father as being worthy of obedience and honor. This is one evidence of the divine origin of the law. In the text just quoted the mother is placed even before the father, perhaps because the earliest part of the training is chiefly hers.

The boy who learns to honor his mother in the home will respect womanhood everywhere. It is sometimes said that Christianity has emancipated womanhood, but the seed of this emancipation proclamation is in the bosom of the decalogue. We read again in the Mosaic writings, *"For everyone that curseth his father or his mother shall be surely put to death: he hath cursed his father or his mother; his blood shall be upon him."* **Leviticus 20:9.** (See also **Exodus 21:17.**) *"Cursed be he that setteth light by his father or his mother."* **Deuteronomy 27:16.**

Children make light of their parents and show them disrespect and dishonor by speaking of them as "the old man" or "the old woman," or by other terms unbecoming to dutiful and respectful children. This is also true when they make light of their clothes, conduct, or lack of culture and education. The wise man said, *"Whoso curseth his father or his mother, his lamp shall be put out in obscure darkness."* **Proverbs 20:20.**

Although this threat doubtless has special reference to the final fate of transgressors, it also is fulfilled to a remarkable extent in this life. Those who dishonor father and mother will sooner or later come to a bad end. Their boasted light will go out in obscurity. Many a sorrowful parent in old age cries out in bitter anguish, *"I have nourished and brought up children, and they have rebelled against me."* Isaiah 1:2.

Many are the gray heads that are brought down in sorrow to premature graves because of disobedient and rebellious children. A profusion of beautiful and expensive flowers together with many tears and demonstrations of grief at the funeral can never atone for willful neglect. David pampered and spoiled his son Absalom, who came to an untimely end and brought forth the cry of anguish from a brokenhearted father, *"O my son Absalom, O Absalom, my son, my son!"* 2 Samuel 19:4. The proper discipline in earlier life would have averted this tragic experience.

No one dare say that the fifth commandment became obsolete and is ignored in the New Testament or was abrogated by Christ at the cross. Like all the other commands of the decalogue, the fifth is emphasized and enforced by New Testament teachings and examples. The second Adam did not come into the world as did the first Adam, a full-grown man, but as a babe who had to grow to manhood under the guardianship of parents, so as to be our example through all the experiences of life from the cradle to the grave. Greater emphasis could not be given to the importance of the fifth commandment than that given by the life and teachings of Jesus.

The experience recorded in **Luke 2:41-52**, when Jesus made His first visit to Jerusalem, shows a very close relationship between Him and His parents. Jesus' answer to the anxious inquiry of His mother as to why He had thus dealt with them was in no wise disrespectful. There is no evidence whatever of a breaking away from parental control. In fact the statement, *"He went down with them, and came to Nazareth, and was subject unto them,"* indicates complete subjection to parental authority.

While the years of direct control and obedience ended with the beginning of His public ministry, Jesus did not cease to honor His mother and provide for her needs. In fact, one of His last acts while enduring the agony of the cross was to make provision for the future care of His mother as long as she lived. (See **John 19:26,27.**)

Jesus also magnified the fifth commandment in His teaching. He severely rebuked the scribes and Pharisees for making void the fifth commandment by their tradition which made it possible for a person to escape responsibility to parents by dedicating his property to the temple or to religious purposes. (See **Matthew 15:1-9.**) It is therefore better to use property in providing for the needs of parents in their old age than to give it to the Lord's work to their neglect. Of course this must not be used as an excuse for not fulfilling our obligations to the Lord in supporting His worldwide gospel work. The statement of Jesus, *"In vain they do worship Me, teaching for doctrines the commandments of men,"* shows that in principle all the commandments are violated by those who break the fifth. It is always true that *"whosoever shall keep the whole law, and yet offend in one point, he is guilty of all."* James 2:10.

In **Ephesians 6:1-3**, which was previously quoted, Paul indicates that it will go ill with children who do not obey the fifth commandment. **"For this is right,"** is the reason given as to why children should obey their parents. Like all the commandments of the law, the fifth is founded on an eternal principle of righteousness that is inherent in the nature of both God and man. Some things are right because they are commanded, and others are commanded because they are right. The first is true of many civil laws, and the latter, of the commands of God. Submission of children to parental law is the logical and natural thing.

Again Paul says, *"Children, obey your parents, in all things: for this is well pleasing unto the Lord."* Colossians 3:20. *"In all things"* is, of course, limited to the things that are right. Parents have no right to command their children to commit sins or crimes. Obedience to the Lord is the first duty even of children. (See **Matthew 10:37.**) Obedience *"in all things"* in order to be *"well pleasing unto the Lord"* must be *"in the Lord."* Why does the Lord seem to delight in filial obedience? Because such conduct sets forth His own virtue and is the soul and law of all His own actions:

The obligations of children to parents and grandparents is again set forth in **1 Timothy 5:4**: *"If a widow has children or grandchildren, let these learn first to show piety towards their own homes and to prove their gratitude to their parents; for this is well pleasing in the sight of God."* (Weymouth translation.) Parents who spend their lives in service for their children when they are young, deserve a recompense from the children when they are old.

"Disobedient to parents" is one of the nineteen sins for which *"the last days"* are designated as *"perilous times"* in 2 Timothy 3:1-5. Being *"without natural affection,"* last-generation children will be *"unthankful"* and *"unholy."* It is evident that all the sins listed in this scripture are the direct and indirect results of home conditions. The home becomes the incubator of sin and the breeding place of crime. Children beginning such a course in the high chair and remaining unchecked, end their careers in the electric chair.

PARENTAL RESPONSIBILITY

It is evident from Hebrews 12:5-12 that the discipline and training of children should be patterned after the Lord's dealings with His children, whom He chastens because of His love so that they *"might be partakers of His holiness."* The fifth commandment presupposes a careful example on the part of parents so that they will deserve honor and respect. Parents should ever remember that a correct example is always more powerful for good than precepts. The honor parents receive from their children depends to a large extent on their own conduct and discipline. The more honorable parents are, the more honor they will receive.

> *"Nothing is more certain than the fact, that, if parents are to be honored, they must be honorable. If obedience is to be rendered gladly and implicitly, it must be to a control that is conditioned in love. Love that is Godlike, farseeing, and comprehensive, love which permits of no present pleasure at the cost of possible future pain; such love can only be where character is in harmony with the divine intention. No father or mother can think right thoughts or plan pure programs for their children unless they, in their turn, are living the life of subjection to God, and are receiving from Him the ordering of all their ways."*
>
> –G. CAMPBELL MORGAN,
> *The Ten Commandments*, pp. 58, 59.

All authority, including that of parents, has its origin and source with God, and is only delegated to those in positions of leadership in all the relationships and institutions of men. Children must be taught to respect the authority of God as exercised through parents, for those who never learn obedience to parental law cannot be expected to respect divine law. Only those who learn to obey are qualified to rule. Only those who accept discipline can properly minister discipline to others. Home government is therefore the cornerstone of national government. The peace and prosperity of a nation depend upon the recognition of constituted authority through discipline in the home.

At no time in life can men and women do as they please, and the earlier that fact is learned, the better for the individual. Although the power of love is greater than the rule of the rod, when either children or adults spurn the overtures of love and the appeals to reason, methods of physical force are the only alternative in the family, school, or state governments. It is still a true saying that *"he that spareth his rod hateth his son: but he that loveth him chasteneth him betimes."* **Proverbs 13:24.** The divinely inspired instruction to parents is, *"Chasten thy son while there is hope, and let not thy soul spare for his crying."* **Proverbs 19:18.** This text indicates that when the child reaches a certain age it is too late to chastise him, because the character has already been formed and fixed. The period when discipline is needed, begins and passes much sooner than most parents realize. In the majority of cases the discipline is delayed too long, if administered at all.

WARNING TO PARENTS

The Scriptures also contain timely counsel to parents in their dealings with the children, *"Ye fathers, provoke not your children to wrath: but bring them up in the nurture and admonition of the Lord." "Fathers, provoke not your children to anger, lest they be discouraged."* **Ephesians 6:4; Colossians 3:21.** *"Nurture"* in the Greek is *"discipline,"* or training by necessary chastening. *"Admonition"* means *"training by counsel."* Both are needed. *"Nurture them in the chastening and admonition of the Lord,"* is the reading of the American Revised Version.

"Provoke" means to irritate or exasperate through unreasonable demands, outbursts of anger, or constant nagging. On the other hand, children can also be ruined by overindulgence and misplaced sympathy. Parents who slave for their children, and thus give them too much attention, invariably spoil them. The more children are made to wait on themselves and others, especially their parents, the better for them. They should also be taught early to entertain

themselves and provide their own amusements. Nothing is more pleasing and agreeable than retiring, unselfish, and unspoiled children; and nothing is more obnoxious and distasteful than bold, self-centered, empty-headed, and parent-pampered children.

Parents should make every effort to make the home the center of attraction for their children. This, of course, is impossible with mere ornamentation and rich furnishings. It comes only by the cultivation of affection, courtesy, comradeship, and the other graces of true Christianity. These alone can make the home the most desirable place on earth. Such a home is a part of heaven because it is filled with the heavenly atmosphere of love, harmony, and fellowship. When love is the abiding and controlling principle of the home, it will be the most wonderful place in the world.

Said the apostle Paul: *"Love is patient and kind. Love knows neither envy nor jealousy. Love is not forward and self-assertive, nor boastful and conceited. She does not behave unbecomingly, nor seek to aggrandize herself, nor blaze out in passionate anger, nor brood over wrongs. She finds no pleasure in injustice done to others, but joyfully sides with the truth. She knows how to be silent. She is full of trust, full of hope, full of patient endurance. Love never fails." "And so there remain faith, hope, love-these three; and of these the greatest is love."* 1 Corinthians 13:4-8, 13, Weymouth.

This surely is a heavenly state, and children reared in such an atmosphere will never fail their parents or their God.

THE DIVINE PROMISE

The promise is, *"Train up a child in the way he should go: and when he is old, he will not depart from it."* Proverbs 22:6. This promise is definite and has but one condition to its fulfillment. The child must be trained *"in the way he should go."* Not in the way he would go or in the way he wants to go, but in the way he should go. *"As the twig is bent the tree's inclined,"* is a no more fixed and unchangeable rule than that which is enunciated in this text. If it does not always seem to work out that way, the promise should not be blamed. No parent is perfect, and therefore cannot do a perfect job of child training, and most parents come farther short of the mark than they realize or are willing to acknowledge. It is safer and wiser to blame ourselves rather than the promise of God.

90

Perhaps among the best examples of success and failure in child training are those of Joseph and Absalom. Joseph made full provision for his father in his old age. He was not ashamed to bring him to Egypt and introduce him to the king. He honored his father through life and his memory after death. But Absalom broke his father's heart when he rebelled and attempted to seize his throne. He was petted and pampered as a boy, and therefore was a dishonor to his parents when he became a man. To this day the Jews throw stones at the monument of Absalom as an evidence of their feeling of disgust. May these two examples be a worthy pattern and a solemn warning to parents in this willful and stubborn generation. No, the fifth commandment is not obsolete or out of date. It has not been superseded by a better code for the conduct of the family government. It only needs to be given a fair trial to demonstrate its value.

THE SACREDNESS OF
HUMAN LIFE

8

"Thou shalt not kill."** **Exodus 20:13.** The sixth commandment is closely related to the fifth and logically follows it. The fifth deals with the home, the place where life has its origin and is developed. It throws a wall of protection around the family, the beginning of all human relationships. The sixth commandment sets forth the sacredness of human life by protecting and safeguarding it. Because man is of divine origin he is under the sovereignty of the Creator, and his life is a part of God's eternal purpose. As the author of life, God alone can know its value.

Since all life comes from the Creator in whom *"we live, and move, and have our being,"* He alone has the right to withdraw it. The consequences of death are so great and so far beyond the comprehension of man that it would be impossible for him to administer it properly to a fellow creature except under the direction of God. Science has utterly failed in all its efforts to create life or understand its mystery. Before this unfathomable secret the greatest sages of all time have stood baffled, in silent wonder.

Life on this earth manifests itself in three realms -the vegetable kingdom, the animal kingdom, and the kingdom of man. All three of these forms of life come from God and are incomprehensible and unexplainable. Nature is filled with mysteries which science is unable to fathom, and with questions that cannot be answered by finite man. The self-propagation of vegetable life and its development from little seeds or roots into plants and trees which produce the necessities of life for birds, beasts, and mankind, are mysteries beyond the ken of the human mind. The wonder increases as we look at the animal kingdom, which climaxes in human life, before which we stand in reverent awe.

The sixth commandment of the decalogue is doubtless designed to protect life in all its forms, but its chief application is to human life. Although both animal and human life are sustained wholly by vegetable life, which must die in order that the higher forms of life may continue, the Scriptures teach that neither vegetable nor animal life should be unnecessarily wasted. Notwithstanding all the modern efforts to preserve and lengthen human life, the world in general places a low value on it, chiefly because it fails to recognize its divine origin and sacredness. The only answer to the origin and meaning of life is to be found in the Sacred Scriptures, and those who reject or neglect this divine revelation will fail to recognize its importance and sacredness. The greatest evidence of the value of human life was the coming of the Son of God into the world to answer the question, *"What is man, that Thou art mindful of him? and the son of man, that Thou visitest him?"* The value of anything is indicated by the price paid for its possession, and Christ paid the supreme price for man's redemption.

THE COMMAND

"Thou shalt do no murder" is the Revised Version rendering, and *"You shall not murder"* is the James Moffatt translation. The **Cambridge Bible** declares that *"the Hebrew word implies violent, unauthorized killing."* The sixth commandment forbids the taking of human life because of enmity or hatred. It includes any human life, whether it be our own or that of a fellow being. Man is forbidden to take the life of another either directly or indirectly, either as Cain slew Abel or as David murdered Uriah. The very fact that it is necessary for the Lord to command us not to kill ourselves or others is evidence of the depravity of human nature and the depth to which man has fallen under the curse of sin.

Life is the gift of God, and man has no right to take what he cannot restore. Neither the continuance nor the cessation of life is within the province of man. He must not kill, because he has no power to restore life or undo the act of killing. As far as man is concerned death is final. Murder is also satanic, for the devil was *"a murderer from the beginning"* and is responsible for the first murder at the gates of Paradise, and for every death that has occurred since.

93

WHAT IS NOT COMMANDED

"Murder" is a better translation than *"kill,"* for it is impossible even to live without killing. All life owes its existence and continuance to death, as is indicated all through the realm of nature. Life in the animal kingdom is sustained wholly by the death of fellow creatures or the taking of life in the vegetable kingdom. If this command prohibited all killing, strict obedience to it would produce starvation.

We know that the sixth commandment cannot forbid the taking of animal life for food, clothing, or other useful purposes. To Noah the Lord said, *"Every moving thing that liveth shall be meat for you; even as the green herb have I given you all things."* **Genesis 9:3**. The Lord commanded His people to kill thousands of animals and birds for sacrificial purposes, and Christ made arrangements for the killing of the Passover lamb, and partook of its flesh with His disciples in the upper room. Although the necessary taking of animal life is allowed, waste of this form of life and unnecessary cruelty are prohibited. Many believe that the Scriptures forbid the taking of animal life for mere sport. Cruelty in the treatment of domestic animals is proscribed in the statement, *"A righteous man regardeth the life of his beast."* **Proverbs 12:10**.

CAPITAL PUNISHMENT

The death penalty for the crime of murder is not a violation of the sixth commandment. The Lord has delegated the power of life and death to civil governments to protect the good and restrain the evil. The Lord says: *"Surely your blood of your lives will I require; at the hand of every beast will I require it, and at the hand of man; at the hand of every man's brother will I require the life of man. Whoso sheddeth man's blood, by man shall his blood be shed: for in the image of God made He man."* **Genesis 9:5, 6**. (See also **Exodus 21:12, 14**.)

This divine rule was given centuries before the existence of the nation of Israel with its national and ceremonial laws. It points back to and is based on the act of creation. The reason given is just as true and valid today. The taking of human life with malicious intent should be punished with death, for "in the image of God created He him." It is because human life is valuable and sacred. First of all, murder is sin against God, for not only is man created in the image of God but he is God's possession by right of creation. The same principle is set forth in the New Testament. Speaking of civil governments which are *"ordained of God"* and civil rulers who are the ministers of God, the apostle Paul wrote, *"But if thou do that which is evil, be afraid; for he beareth not the sword in vain: for he is the minister of God, a revenger to execute wrath upon him that doeth evil."* Romans 13:4. The bearing of the sword indicates the power to execute the sentence of death. The right and duty of capital punishment is of divine origin and sanction, and the legal execution of the death penalty is not murder.

UNINTENTIONAL KILLING

That it is possible to kill human beings without being guilty of breaking the sixth commandment is evident from the provision the Lord made for the protection of those guilty of unintentional slayings done *"unawares"* or *"unwittingly,"* or without malice afore thought on the part of the slayer. In the city of refuge the slayer was safe from *"the avenger of blood"* until it was established whether the crime was premeditated or unintentional. If the murder was premeditated, the criminal was denied the sanctuary and was delivered to his pursuers to be put to death. If investigation showed that the crime was without intent to kill, the accuser was permitted to remain in the place of safety. Although deprived of his full liberty till the death of the reigning high priest, he was safe as long as he remained in the refuge city. (See **Numbers 35**.)

This shows that the Lord recognizes a distinction between mere killing and murder. The statement of Christ to Peter, *"Put up again thy sword into his place: for all they that take the sword shall perish with the sword"* (**Matthew 26:52**), is sometimes used as an argument against capital punishment. The fact is that it proves exactly the opposite. Jesus never spoke contrary to His own laws found in the Old Testament. The person who wields the sword against his neighbor must himself suffer the same penalty by the same weapon. He who ministers death must suffer death. This is the divine law.

SELF-MURDER

It is evident that suicide, or self-murder, is included in the prohibition of the sixth commandment. God is the giver and owner of human life by right of creation. Also, we are His by right of redemption. Paul declares that we are not our own but have been *"bought with a price."* Suicide is worse than the murder of another because of the fact that the self-murderer has no opportunity to repent of his sin, and we are clearly told that *"no murderer hath eternal life abiding in him."* 1 John 3:15. *"Do thyself no harm,"* was the command of Paul to the Philippian jailer who was in the act of taking his own life. (**Acts 16:28.**)

There are more than ten thousand suicides a year in this country, and this crime is rapidly increasing among all classes and in all lands. Suicide is a cowardly act to escape what braver men and women patiently bear. Plato said it was a desertion of the post of duty. The Bible records only four suicides, and none of them were good men. They are King Saul; his armor-bearer; Ahithophel, the fellow conspirator with Absalom; and Judas Iscariot, the betrayer of Jesus.

INDIRECT MURDER

In the crime of criminal carelessness or negligence, the party responsible for the crime is just as guilty as if he had perpetrated it himself. This also is a divinely given rule: *"If an ox gore a man or woman, that they die: then the ox shall be surely stoned, and his flesh shall not be eaten; but the owner of the ox shall be quit. But if the ox were wont to push with his horn in time past, and it hath been testified to his owner, and he hath not kept him in, but that he hath killed a man or a woman; the ox shall be stoned, and his owner also shall be put to death."* Exodus 21: 28, 29.

Likewise the person who plans a crime and gets others to commit it for him is, if possible, more guilty than the person who does the actual deed. David was more of a murderer than Joab and his soldiers who executed his orders to bring about the death of Uriah. Through the prophet Nathan the Lord said to David: *"Wherefore hast thou despised the commandment of the LORD, to do evil in His sight? thou hast killed Uriah the Hittite with the sword, and hast taken his wife to be thy wife, and hath slain him with the sword of the children of Ammon. Now therefore the sword shall never depart from thine house."* 2 Samuel 12: 9, 10.

MURDER BY DEGREES

It is possible to kill ourselves by degrees through indulgences and dissipations that are known to be injurious to health. Anything that shortens our own life or the lives of others is a form of suicide and murder. Any pleasure or indulgence engaged in at the price of premature death is a sin included in the sixth commandment. Millions of people who would be shocked at the very thought of suicide or murder are engaged in the prolonged process of self-murder and are digging their own graves with their teeth. Their appetites and passions are killing them. Thousands are carrying on a conscious program of slow suicide and are making no effort to check it.

It is a Christian duty to become acquainted with the laws of health and to obey them to the best of one's ability. Appetite is a means to an end and should never be made the end itself. We should eat to live and not live to eat. The sixth command goes with us to the table. It commends and commands practices that produce health and long life and condemns those that impair health and shorten life. It condemns all needless physical risks. In fact, the whole broad subject of healthful living is embraced in the sixth commandment. Like all the other commands, the sixth is *"exceeding broad,"* so that the ten embrace *"the whole duty of man."*

MOST POPULAR FORM OF MURDER

Someone has truly said that *"hate is murder on the way, just as lust is adultery begun, and covetousness is theft in embryo."* We are told that Jesus came to *"magnify the law,"* and **Matthew 5:21-26** is the sixth commandment under the magnifying glass of spiritual illumination. The Master declared that anger and hatred, which contain the spirit and seeds of murder, make one a potential murderer. The apostle said, *"Whosoever hateth his brother is a murderer: and ye know that no murderer hath eternal life abiding in him."* 1 John 3:15.

This language cannot well be misunderstood. These texts track murder to its very source. Not alone the fatal blow that strikes down the victim, but also the angry passion that prompts the blow is forbidden. Anger is dangerous, because it eventually hardens into hatred, and the hater is a potential murderer.

It is always proper to hate iniquity provided we love righteousness. Hateful and malicious words are the first weapon used by selfish anger, and they produce deep and deadly, though bloodless, wounds. The uncontrolled tongue *"is an unruly evil, full of deadly poison."* James 3:8. It is as murderous as a sharp sword, a piercing arrow, or a speeding bullet. It cuts and slashes its victims with murderous intent and purpose. The tongue is the great character assassin, and what form of murder could be more serious in its consequences than that which destroys the character, which alone can take us into the life that is eternal?

THE POSITIVE PHASE

The positive phase of the sixth commandment is, "**Thou shalt love thy neighbor as thyself.**" It requires that we have our neighbor's interests at heart so that we seek his welfare. We are not only to refrain from injuring or killing him or even shortening his life, but we are also to practice the golden rule in all our dealings with our fellow men, including our enemies. Jesus said: *"Love your enemies, bless them that curse you, do good to them that hate you, and pray for them which despitefully use you, and persecute you; that ye may be the children of your Father which is in heaven: for He maketh His sun to rise on the evil and on the good, and sendeth rain on the just and on the unjust."* Matthew 5:44, 45.

The apostle Paul said, *"Therefore if thine enemy hunger, feed him; if he thirst, give him drink: for in so doing thou shalt heap coals of fire on his head."* Romans 12:20. This is the sixth commandment in the positive; it is Christianity in action. This precept not only refrains from evil; it also enjoins righteousness, for, says the psalmist, *"All Thy commandments are righteousness."* May this commandment with all its breadth be written on the fleshy tables of our hearts so that we will be living epistles *"known and read of all men."*

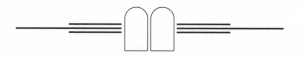

THE SACREDNESS OF MARRIAGE

9

"*T hou shalt not commit adultery.*" **Exodus 20:14**. The first three commands of the second table of the decalogue, which deals with human relationships, are in their proper order. This table begins at the fifth commandment, with the home, the place where life and its relationships have their origin, and in the sixth, the sacredness of human life is then safeguarded. But life exists in two sexes or forms-the male and the female-in order that life may perpetuate itself through successive generations.

The seventh command therefore throws a guard around marriage, the most intimate, binding, and sacred of all human relationships, and the one on which the very existence and perpetuity of the race depends.

The sacredness of the marriage institution depends on the safeguarding of morals in all the experiences and relationships of life between the cradle and the grave. The prohibitions of the seventh commandment are therefore *"exceeding broad."* In language and spirit it prohibits all forms of moral uncleanness in word, thought, or conduct, both before and after marriage. Immorality in all its forms is just as much a sin before marriage as is unfaithfulness afterward. The law and the gospel demand purity of all who have been created in the image of God. It has been truthfully said that *"virtue, the strength and beauty of the soul, is the best gift of Heaven,"* and also that *"virtue alone is happiness below."*

Physical passions constitute an important part of human nature, and, like many of the elements in nature, are valuable servants but terrible masters. Impurity is the master sin of the human race and the most dreadful of all in its consequences. Fornication not only demands a terrible toll in this life but also excludes one from the life to come. Made in the image of God, men and women are under the most solemn obligation to preserve unmarred the divine image of their Maker, in its moral as well as its physical aspect.

The marriage institution is of divine origin and is an important part of the divine plan and purpose. It should never be entered into without a recognition of God. Morality and religion cannot be separated, and therefore, because of its origin and significance, the divine element of marriage should never be forgotten. The law that safeguards marriage is a divine law, and it is always dangerous to violate a divine law or tamper with a divine institution.

Marriage is still further ennobled by the fact that it has been chosen as the symbol of the sacred union between Christ and His church. Throughout both the Old and the New Testament, Christ is represented as the husband and bridegroom, and the church as His wife or bride.

ADULTERY DEFINED

This commandment prohibits all immoral relations between the sexes, and since the illicit act is the result of evil thinking, it also forbids mental uncleanness and lustful looks. Adultery is unfaithfulness to the marriage relationship on the part of either husband or wife, whereas fornication embraces all kinds of unlawful sex behavior before or after marriage. Adultery is the breaking of a most solemn vow and the betrayal of a most sacred trust. It is dishonesty in the most sacred and binding of all the relationships of life. It is a crime against oneself, one's companion, the church, society, the nation, and against God. It is the selling of one's moral birthright for a mess of sensual pottage with a lifetime of regrets. We have reached the anti-type of the days of Noah, when *"the wickedness of man was great in the earth"* and when *"every imagination of the thoughts of the heart was only evil continually."* Genesis 6:5. The modern generation needs to be gathered at the base of the mount of the law to again hear the decree of the Almighty, *"Thou shalt not commit adultery."*

SIN AGAINST NATURE

Fornication is a sin against nature, and it is therefore unnatural. Nature demands absolute purity and exacts a terrible toll for the violation of her laws, and in no realm is the penalty more severe than in regard to sex. For the immoral, nature has no pity or mercy.

The seventh commandment demands personal purity in thought and deed. It prohibits those secret personal vices among both men and women that debase the mind, undermine the health, and pollute the soul. Of these *"unfruitful works of darkness"* Paul says that *"it is a shame even to speak of those things which are done of them in secret."* Ephesians 5:11, 12.

The seriousness of the sin of immorality against our own or the bodies of others is set forth in **1 Corinthians 6:15-20**: *"Know ye not that your bodies are the members of Christ? shall I then take the members of Christ, and make them the members of an harlot? God forbid. What? know ye not that he which is joined to an harlot is one body? for two, said he, shall be one flesh. But he that is joined unto the Lord is one spirit. Flee fornication. Every sin that a man doeth is without the body; but he that committeth fornication sinneth against his own body. What? know ye not that your body is the temple of the Holy Ghost which is in you, which ye have of God, and ye are not your own? For ye are bought with a price: therefore glorify God in your body, and in your spirit, which are God's."*

All other sins are external, but this one is a sin against nature. It pollutes the body, *"the temple of the Holy Ghost,"* and makes the fornicator one flesh with the harlot. It is for this reason that moral unfaithfulness is made the only justifiable reason for divorce and remarriage.

Fornication is not only a sin against nature, or a personal sin; it is also a sin against society. Any social or political philosophy that seeks to interfere with the sanctity of family life must eventually bring social and national ruin. The chief cause of the fall of Babylon, Greece, and Rome, was moral degeneracy rather than superior military power arrayed against them. They fell to pieces because of their inward rottenness. The antediluvian world was destroyed and Sodom and Gomorrah were turned to ashes because of licentiousness. The modern nations are fast rushing toward the same doom. Immorality is a racial sin. No other sin is handed down to future generations as is licentiousness. It is a sin against the human race, because it affects more than the original sinners. It affects the inheritance of unborn generations.

NEW TESTAMENT TEACHING

The emphasis given to the seventh commandment in the New Testament shows that it was not abrogated by Christ or set aside by the apostles. Like the other commandments of the decalogue, the binding claims of the seventh are strengthened and established by the gospel. In the sermon on the mount Jesus magnified the meaning of immorality to include the thoughts and motives. He said, *"Ye have heard that it was said by them of old time, Thou shalt not commit adultery: but I say unto you, That whosoever looketh on a woman to lust after her hath committed adultery with her already in his heart."* Matthew 5:27, 28.

Jesus then declared that it would be better to pluck out a lustful eye or cut off an offending hand rather than to be cast into hell because of licentious habits. He goes to the very heart of this question by making it plain that a clean mind is the only hope of a clean life. He shows that the person who looks upon the opposite sex with longing desire for impure relations is already guilty of fornication. The seventh commandment may be transgressed by evil imaginations. In fact, this is the form in which it is most frequently violated in this evil-minded generation.

On another occasion Jesus said, *"Out of the heart proceed evil thoughts, murders, adulteries, fornications, thefts, false witness, blasphemies: these are the things which defile a man."* Matthew 15:19, 20. The place to conquer this sin, as well as all others, is at its fountain, before it becomes a physical act. Jesus taught that these impure thoughts and desires which reach the stage of lust are not only wrong because they lead to sin but they are also sin in themselves. The temptation itself is not sin, but when the impure desire is welcomed and harbored and only the lack of opportunity prevents it from becoming an act, it is adultery.

That lust is the motive power of all evil is evident from 1 John 2:15-17: *"Love not the world, neither the things that are in the world. If any man love the world, the love of the Father is not in him. For all that is in the world, the lust of the flesh, and the lust of the eyes, and the pride of life, is not of the Father, but is of the world. And the world passeth away, and the lust thereof: but he that doeth the will of God abideth forever."*

Here we are given the three sources of all temptations through which the wicked one entices to sin. In James 1:14, 15 we are told just when temptation becomes a sin: *"Every man is tempted, when he is drawn away of his own lust, and enticed. Then when lust hath conceived, it bringeth forth sin: and sin, when it is finished, bringeth forth death."* When the mind consents to the evil suggestion so that only the absence of opportunity prevents it from becoming a deed, the conception takes place that gives birth to sin.

Lust is the devil's counterfeit of love. Nothing is more uplifting and beautiful than love, and nothing more degrading and blighting than lust. Lust soon destroys all natural affection and leaves the heart and soul destitute of all that is noble and virtuous. Since the evil of fornication begins with wrong thinking, we should discipline our minds to habits of clean thoughts and carefully avoid the first step toward this sin of sins. *"Be not conformed to this world: but be ye transformed by the renewing of your mind"* is good advice. (Romans 12:2.) The divine promise is, *"Blessed is the man that endureth temptation: for when he is tried, he shall receive the crown of life, which the Lord hath promised to them that love Him."* James 1:12.

THE PENALTY

Perhaps no other sin visits upon the transgressor a more severe penalty, both in this life and in the judgment, than fornication. It is *"the way to hell, going down to the chambers of death."* Proverbs 7: 27. One who passed through the experience of bitter remorse declared that the wages of this sin is *"many times worse than death."* The wise man said that this sin *"hath cast many down wounded: yea, many strong men have been slain by her."* Proverbs 7:26. Samson and David are among the *"strong men"* slain or wounded by this terrible sin.

The following is another terrible warning against this universal sin: *"By means of a whorish woman a man is brought to a piece of bread: and the adulteress will hunt for the precious life. Can a man take fire into his bosom, and his clothes not be burned?... So he that goeth in to his neighbor's wife; whosoever toucheth her shall not be innocent.... Whoso committeth adultery with a woman lacketh understanding: he that doeth it destroyeth his own soul. A wound and dishonor shall he get; and his reproach shall not be wiped away."* **Proverbs 6:26-33.** The truthfulness of this last statement is emphasized by the everlasting reproach of David, which the Lord said would continue through all human history. His sin was forgiven, but the reproach continues.

The apostle Paul said, *"Be not deceived: neither fornicators, nor idolaters, nor adulterers, nor effeminate, nor abusers of themselves with mankind... shall inherit the kingdom of God."* **1 Corinthians 6:9, 10.** (See also **Ephesians 5:3-7.**) In **Revelation 21:8** we are told that *"whoremongers"* are among those who will *"have their part in the lake which burneth with fire and brimstone: which is the second death."* Our reformatories, penitentiaries, and insane asylums are filled with those who feel the sting of the penalty of the sin of fornication.

THE REMEDY

For this sin, as for all save one, there is a remedy. Better still there is victory for those who are tempted. In repentance, confession, and a determination to sin no more, there is pardon, cleansing, and acceptance, although the ugly scar is carried through life. David found this remedy, and had created in him *"a clean heart"* and *"a right spirit,"* although he bore the reproach of his sin as long as he lived. Jesus said to the repentant, wicked woman, *"Thy sins are forgiven. . . Thy faith hath saved thee; go in peace"* (Luke 7: 48-50), and to the woman taken in adultery, *"Neither do I condemn thee; go, and sin no more."* John 8:11.

A preventive is always better than a remedy. Through the power of an indwelling Christ we may be kept from failing. The most outstanding example of victory over the sin of immorality recorded in the Scriptures is that of Joseph when tempted by the designing wife of Potiphar. He met the temptation of this siren of licentiousness with the statement, *"How then can I do this great wickedness, and sin against God?"* He repelled her further advances and thus incurred her wrath, and in order to avenge wounded pride she sent him to prison through her lies. But he maintained his integrity and was eventually richly rewarded.

SAFEGUARD TO MARRIAGE

The seventh commandment throws a bulwark around marriage and the home in order to guard from pollution the fountain from which flows the stream of life. All forms of moral uncleanness defile this stream and affect the marriage institution. In his book *The Ten Commandments,* page 91, **Ferdinand S. Schenck** said:

"A high ideal of marriage is a great incentive to purity of heart. If young people anticipate a pure marriage every step toward it must be in the way of virtue. If you wish to win a pure white soul for your life-long companion you will be unwilling to give less than you wish to receive. You will keep your own soul white and clean."

The foundation of many a marriage is ruined before the union is consummated at the altar. True marriage is a life partnership for a noble purpose and does not depend so much on physical attractions as on beauty of character. Perfect mutual trust is essential to a happy marriage, and the confidence in each other must be so complete that it banishes all curiosity about the details of each other's private affairs. True love never enslaves, nor does it destroy individuality or the power of choice.

Marriage, in order to be successful, must be consummated *"in the Lord,"* or according to His will, which always excludes the marriage of a Christian with an unbeliever. *"Be ye not unequally yoked together with unbelievers"* is a divine command. (2 Corinthians 6:14.) When *"God hath joined together"* the man and woman, *"marriage is honorable in all, and the bed undefiled."* Hebrews 13:4.

THE DIVORCE EVIL

Lax divorce laws constitute one of the worst enemies of the marriage institution. They have lowered the general estimate of the sacredness of marriage and created heedlessness in regard to its binding claims. Our easy divorce laws have made possible "a species of consecutive polygamy." In the early days of the Roman Republic there were no divorces, because the sanctity of family life was recognized. Rome fell when the home was undermined and divorce became common, just as any structure will collapse when its foundation gives way. The American Republic is fast following in the footsteps of Rome, and the same causes will produce the same results. When marriage is based on human emotions, heedless impulse, heartless convenience, or romantic adventure, rather than love founded on character, the results can be nothing short of domestic tragedy. Between one third and one half of the marriages in this country are now ending in the divorce courts, and in some sections the number of divorces exceeds the marriages.

The opinion seems to prevail that in Old Testament times divorce was divinely sanctioned on other than the ground of fornication, but this is a false idea. It is true that the Pharisees tempted Christ with the question, *"Is it lawful for a man to put away his wife?"* The answer of Jesus was, *"What did Moses command you?"* The Pharisees replied that Moses permitted a bill of divorcement, which Jesus said was done because of the hardness of their hearts. (See **Mark 10:2-6.**)

We must ever remember that the Old and New Testaments came from the same source, and they therefore cannot contradict each other. Jesus only magnified the law, and that which is magnified has nothing altered by way of subtraction or addition. Jesus said: *"It hath been said, Whosoever shall put away his wife, let him give her a writing of divorcement: but I say unto you, That whosoever shall put away his wife, saving for the cause of fornication, causeth her to commit adultery: and whosoever shall marry her that is divorced committeth adultery."* Matthew 5:31, 32.

The instructions of Jesus during His sermon on the mount were exactly the same as those He gave to ancient Israel through Moses. The scriptures in both testaments teach that marriage is permanent and that its ties are so binding that they can be broken only by death, or its equivalent-that which is far worse than death-moral delinquency on the part of husband or wife, or both. The Bible recognizes but one cause for divorce and remarriage, and the church dare not alter the Word by becoming more stringent or more lenient in dealing with offenders.

Of course, when the divorce and remarriage have taken place before those concerned made a profession of Christianity and while they were ignorant of their sin, this sin, with all others previously committed, is washed away in the blood of Christ and their past lives are covered with His righteousness. The Lord takes people where He finds them, and there are many things in their past that never can be undone without committing an even greater sin. But this excuse cannot be made to apply to church members or those who commit this sin presumptuously. For such persons there can be no remarriage with divine approval.

But when the case is clear that Scriptural grounds exist, the innocent person has just as much right to remarry as he had to enter the first marriage. The innocent one is doubly released by the remarriage of the guilty one, but if both husband and wife are innocent of moral unfaithfulness and separate for other reasons, the remarriage of either party constitutes adultery and releases the other party to remarry without being guilty of transgression. These lofty principles are recognized by all denominations that have any standards left, and the restating of them in this connection does not constitute any private interpretation of the Scriptures on this subject.

There are a number of contributing causes of the present-day increase of moral delinquency and divorce, which belong to this subject. At the head of the list should be placed the modern theater, which has fattened financially on the licentious filth that appeals to the baser instincts of sinful flesh and the carnal nature. **Plato** declared that *"plays rouse the passions and pervert the use of them; and of course, are dangerous to morality,"* and Augustus Caesar was advised by **Ovid** to suppress the theaters because they were *"a grand source of corruption."* **Rousseau** called the theater of his day *"a school of vice,"* and **Macaulay** said it was *"a seminary of vice."*

No person would dare say that the theater has reformed since the days of these men. In fact, plenty of evidence could be produced to show that its influence since the introduction of the moving and talking pictures has become more widespread and dangerous. The ancient theater was attended almost entirely by adults, but the present-day audience is composed largely of children and youth. It is estimated that twenty million of them attend the theaters each day in the United States. All efforts to reform the theater by the introduction of educational and moral plays and pictures have ended in failure, because the majority who patronize this industry demand sex thrills and unclean amusements; and the producers give them what they want, because with them money is more precious than morals.

Another evil influence that is degrading modern morals is the filthy literature that is flooding the world and spilling over into our homes in ever increasing streams which glorify vice and countenance whoremongers and libertines. Much of this literature belittles marriage and speaks disparagingly of the binding claims of the marriage vow. Illicit sex relations are pictured in the most attractive colors, and virtue and moral standards are described as being antiquated and out of date. No young person can live on this sort of mental diet without becoming an easy victim to sensual lust, which will eventually scorch the soul and debase the character. The only safety for the modern youth is to avoid this kind of lewd literature as he would the deadly poison of a rattlesnake, and learn to choose those books and papers that are elevating and ennobling.

"Evil company doth corrupt good manners," is an old Greek proverb quoted by Paul, which sets forth a long-recognized truth. Association with those who indulge in sensual manners, practice undue familiarity, and tell smutty stories, will lead to a lowering of our own ideas of propriety and destroy our faith in the honor of manhood and the virtue of womanhood. It has been said that a person is known by the company he keeps, for each person seeks his own character level. A filthy conversation never comes out of a pure mind and a clean heart. The counsel of Scripture is, *"Let no corrupt communication proceed out of your mouth." "Neither filthiness, nor foolish talking, nor jesting, which are not convenient,"* or becoming. **Ephesians 4:29; 5:4.** The wise man said, *"My son, if sinners entice thee, consent thou not."* **Proverbs 1:10.** *"Flee also youthful lusts"* is the counsel of the apostle Paul.

OTHER CAUSES

Modern dress or undress is also a serious problem that has to do with morals. The present-day mania for nudity is an insult to nature and everything that is beautiful and virtuous. Many today are not satisfied even with the fig-leaf style of covering invented by the first human sinner. The unchaste and lewd in drama and literature and the tendency toward the nude in art and dress indicate that modesty is becoming a lost virtue. The counsel of the Lord through the apostle Paul was never more needed than today: *"I will therefore... that women adorn themselves in modest apparel."* **1 Timothy 2:8, 9.** The cultured Christian woman will avoid all extremes in dress and will keep pace with the sensible fashions of her day.

The modern dance is also contributing to the moral degeneracy of this generation and is the acknowledged cause of many moral tragedies. Investigation has revealed the fact that thousands of those who are inmates of penal and corrective institutions began their career in immorality and crime on the dance floor. Take the mutual attractions of sex out of the dance and it would soon cease to exist.

Intoxicating drinks and various modern drugs tend to inflame the animal passions and weaken resistance to the warnings of reason and conscience. The sum of these enticements to evil have brought us to very perilous and dangerous times when the only safety is a deeply spiritual experience. Without this even a thorough knowledge of truth will not save us from becoming involved in the swirling cesspool of iniquity that is engulfing modern society and making it comparable to the licentious days of Noah and Lot, when destruction was the only remedy. *"Be clean,"* is the command of God to all men, and all His commands are enablings. He never requires the impossible. He furnishes the power to translate His requirements into possibilities and His promises into realities, and the seventh commandment is no exception to this rule.

THE VIRTUE OF HONESTY

10

"*Thou shalt not steal.*" **Exodus 20:15**. The first three of the six commands of the second table of the decalogue have to do with human life itself in both its physical and its moral aspects, whereas the last three deal with and protect man's property. The eighth commandment protects our temporal possessions, the ninth safeguards our names and reputations, and the tenth forbids the covetous spirit that gives birth to stealing.

Under the Mosaic law the penalty for the violation of each of the first seven commandments was death. Although a lesser penalty was imposed for the transgression of the last three commands, the sentence of the heavenly tribunal for all sin is eternal death. But even under Mosaic law the seriousness of the sins of covetousness and stealing is indicated by the divinely imposed sentence of death upon Achan for his covetousness and theft in connection with the capture of Jericho.

The eighth commandment lays down the basic principle on which rests all human legislation for the protection of the rights of property. It is a recognition of the right to possess personal and private property and a prohibition of any violation of that right. The word "*steal*" in its Hebrew original means "*to take by stealth,*" or "*secretly.*" It includes, however, all forms of theft, or the taking of what belongs to another with the intent of keeping it, whether by stealth or by violent attack.

This command, like all others, is written in the very nature of man. The thief himself knows that stealing is wrong, even where there are no written laws to forbid it. Anything of value that is taken from the hand, mind, or heart of another is stealing. Active stealing, in which a person is dispossessed of his goods, and passive stealing, in which a person refuses to give to another what is his by right, are alike condemned by the eighth commandment.

RIGHT OF PROPERTY

To ignore the fundamental right to own and possess property, real or personal, is fatal to both society and government. No genuine Christian can consistently believe in the atheistic and destructive philosophy of socialism or communism, which has no basis whatever in the Scriptures. The patriarchs owned property as did the Israelites after reaching the Promised Land, and many divinely given laws regulated the right of private property and imposed penalties for their violation. Through Peter the Lord told Ananias and Sapphira that their property was their own, to be kept or sold as they chose. Their sin was in lying and in refusing to fulfill their pledge. The so-called communism of apostolic days was wholly voluntary and was confined to the city of Jerusalem. It was practiced but a short time to meet an emergency, and furnishes no basis whatever for modern political communism or socialism.

But human ownership is always limited and secondary. God is the absolute owner of all things. He is the unlimited *"possessor of heaven and earth."* **Genesis 14:19.** To Israel the Lord said, *"All the earth is mine"* (**Exodus 19:5**), and the psalmist said, *"The earth is the LORD's, and the fullness thereof; the world, and they that dwell therein."* **Psalms 24:1.** This text was quoted by Paul in **1 Corinthians 10:96.** (See also **Psalms 50:9-12; Haggai 2:8.**) Man's ownership of property is therefore relative and secondary. He is only a tenant or steward with a definite obligation to the real owner.

The right of individual property, therefore, comes from God and not from the state. It is a divine right based on the authority of the Creator. The dominion of man over all things on earth was a gift from the Eternal. (See **Psalms 8:4-9.**) All that has been lost through sin is to be restored by inheritance through Christ. *"For all things are yours; whether... the world, or life, or death, or things present, or things to come; all are yours; and ye are Christ's; and Christ is God's."* **1 Corinthians 3:21-23.** *"The children of God"* are declared to be *"heirs of God, and joint heirs with Christ,"* in **Romans 8:16, 17.**

111

The evidence by which we recognize that God is the owner of all things and that we are only tenants or stewards is the tithe, and a failure to return to *"the possessor of heaven and earth"* that which He demands as an evidence of His claims of ownership is divinely designated as robbery. (See **Genesis 14:18-20; Malachi 3:7-14.**) Robbing God in tithes and offerings is the most serious of all forms of theft and is a sin of which no Christian should be guilty. It is bad enough to rob our fellow men, but it is far worse to rob our Maker.

STRICT HONESTY

The eighth commandment demands strict honesty in all our dealings with both God and man. It has been truly said that *"an honest man's the noblest work of God."* Both time and experience have proved that *"honesty's the best policy"* at all times and under all circumstances. Its rewards may sometimes be long delayed, but they are certain and enriching in the end. Honesty in business matters demands the giving of an equivalent in time, money, or labor, for what we receive, in all our dealings with others. **Bernard Shaw** once said that *"a gentleman puts more into life than he takes out,"* and the same should be even more true of a Christian.

In all his business transactions the Christian gives *"good measure, pressed down, and shaken together, and running over."* **Luke 6:38.** *"Show me a people whose trade is dishonest, and I will show you a people whose religion is a sham,"* declared **Froude**. Only those who are strictly honest in all their relations with God and man can be saved. Paul said, *"Be not deceived: neither... thieves, nor covetous, nor drunkards, nor revilers, nor extortioners, shall inherit the kingdom of God."* **1 Corinthians 6:9, 10.**

There are only three ways by which we may come into possession of anything: by gift, which includes inheritance; by labor, both mental and physical; and by stealing. The eighth commandment recognizes the right of possession through the first two methods, and prohibits it through the other method. The first two fulfill the law of love and labor, and the third violates it. The thief gets possession of his property by fraud or violence. The two legitimate means of gaining possession of property are commended and the illegitimate way condemned in **Ephesians 4:28:** *"Let him that stole steal no more: but rather let him labor,* *working with his hands the thing which is good, that he may have to give to him that needeth."* Everything possessed by everybody has been received either as a gift or by labor or by theft.

FORMS OF VIOLATION

Theft is one of the most flagrant forms of the violation of this commandment. Its seriousness is enhanced by the fact that theft is usually committed deliberately and as the result of planning. It is seldom the sin of ignorance. It is the unlawful taking of another's goods without his knowledge or consent. Robbery is another form of the sin of stealing. It is taking property or goods by force or violence. Embezzlement is a breach of trust. It is the appropriation to one's own use of money or property held by him in trust for safekeeping. This is the sin of the banker or treasurer of a company when he fraudulently appropriates money of which he is only the custodian. He may intend to pay it back, but if he does he returns stolen money. The sin is in the taking, whether he is caught or not.

The private use of the tithe is clearly a case of embezzlement of the Lord's goods. Because of the faith and trust involved, embezzlement is worse in many respects than robbery. Stealing from the public treasury on the part of those elected to office is a popular form of thievery that totals several billions of dollars a year and which is destroying the confidence of the electorate to the extent that only 50 or 60 per cent of the voters go to the polls in the average election. Stealing from the church treasury is, of course, a still more serious form of embezzlement that will not go unpunished in the day of final reckoning.

Perhaps no form of stealing is more popular in these days than gambling, in its many and varied manifestations. Through betting, lotteries, and all sorts of "skin games," men and women are trying to get something for nothing. These are all forms of theft. Gambling has been called "the new national disease" whose unlawful profits reach the staggering sum of $10,000,000,000 a year in the United States alone. The very least that can be said of a person who obtains money through games of chance is that he is a thief in the making, if he is not one already.

In his book *The Ten Commandments*, **R. E. Golladay** says:

"Gambling stands in about the same relation to stealing as dueling does to murder. Because a man is willing to risk his life in an encounter, does not make it right for him to take another man's life. Nor does the fact that a man is willing to risk his own property in a game of chance, make it right for him to take another man's property without the payment of an equivalent. There is nothing considerate or brotherly in a gambling transaction. Men gamble simply as a result of their feverish desire for quick and easy gain at any cost, even of their souls."

–Page 310.

Extortion is another form of stealing. To Israel the Lord said, **"Thou hast taken usury and increase, and thou hast greedily gained of thy neighbors by extortion, and hast forgotten Me, saith the LORD God."** Ezekiel 22:12. Jesus declared that the Pharisees were *"full of extortion and excess."* **Matthew 23:25.** Paul declared that *"extortioners"* shall not *"inherit the kingdom of God."* **1 Corinthians 6:10.** Extortion is the sin of officials and others who oppress and prey upon the poor by taking advantage of situations that make it possible for them to collect more than is due. This is a popular but serious sin that will not go unpunished by Him who says, **"Vengeance is Mine; I will repay, saith the LORD."**

The sin of extortion is also described in **Leviticus 25:14,** **"If thou sell aught unto thy neighbor, or buyest aught of thy neighbor's hand, ye shall not oppress one another."** It is always wrong to drive a sharp bargain because circumstances place the buyer or seller at your mercy so that you can dictate your own price or terms. Obtaining money under false pretenses is also a form of stealing. This includes lying advertisements in print or over the radio as well as all other forms of stealing "within the law." Jacob was "within the law" when he stole his brother's birthright. He doubtless considered it a shrewd bargain which demonstrated his business ability. Jacob was not punished by the civil authorities because his thievery was "within the law." But later when Laban practiced the same sort of trickery on him, Jacob was indignant and complained bitterly. With such persons it always makes a great difference as to who is being defrauded. **"As the partridge sitteth on eggs, and hatcheth them not; so he that getteth riches, and not by right, shall leave them in the midst of his days, and at his end shall be a fool."** Jeremiah 17:11.

114

EMPLOYERS AND EMPLOYEES

Stealing includes the underpaying of laborers or the withholding of their wages. *"Thou shalt not oppress an hired servant that is poor and needy, whether he be of thy brethren, or of thy strangers that are in thy land within thy gates: at his day thou shalt give him his hire, neither shall the sun go down upon it; for he is poor, and setteth his heart upon it: lest he cry against thee unto the* LORD, *and it be sin unto thee."* Deuteronomy 24:14, 15.

Note other scriptures setting forth the same principles of honesty: *"Thou shalt not defraud thy neighbor, neither rob him: the wage of him that is hired shall not abide with thee all night until the morning."* Leviticus 19:13. *"Woe unto him... that useth his neighbor's service without wages, and giveth him not for his work."* Jeremiah 22:13. *"Behold, the hire of the laborers who have reaped down your fields, which is of you kept back by fraud, crieth: and the cries of them which have reaped are entered into the ears of the Lord of sabaoth."* James 5:4.

These texts demand the strictest honesty on the part of employers. It is not only wrong to withhold wages; it is also wrong to delay payment beyond the time agreed upon. Many professed Christians are guilty of sin on this basis. No employer has the right to take advantage of a situation and pay starvation wages just because the employee cannot help himself. He should be paid what his labor is worth in returns to the employer or business at the time the service is rendered. The eighth commandment forbids overworking and underpaying workers, and it demands a fair deal. *"A fair wage for a fair day's work,"* is a Christian maxim. His service is often all a poor man has to sell, and the man who buys has a God-given duty to treat him justly.

On the other hand, the employee must do a fair day's work and give in service the equivalent of that which he receives in wages, or he, too, is a thief. The man who shirks his duty and loiters on his job and wastes the time for which he is being paid is guilty of violating this command. Many employees deliberately attempt to give just as little labor as possible for the wages received.

The eighth commandment demands economy, diligence, frugality, and industry. The divine command is *"that if any would not work, neither should he eat."* 2 Thessalonians 3:10. The apostle then declared that some were acting *"disorderly, working not at all, but are busybodies.*" He then commanded his class "*that with quietness they work, and eat their own bread.*" This would be wise legislation at the present time. It would do more to end financial depressions than all other experiments combined. The Lord seems to place a special ban on indolence.

The wise man said: "*I went by the field of the slothful, and by the vineyard of the man void of understanding; and, lo, it was all grown over with thorns, and nettles had covered the face thereof, and the stone wall thereof was broken down. Then I saw, and considered it well: I looked upon it, and received instruction. Yet a little sleep, a little slumber, a little folding of the hands to sleep: so shall thy poverty come as one that traveleth; and thy want as an armed man.*" Proverbs 24:30-34.

FRAUDULENT DEALINGS

A business adage of the first century was "*Caveat emptor,*" which means "let the buyer beware." This adage has not become out of date. One writer has said that "*many 'cut-rate stores' should be called 'cut-weight stores'*"; and another said that "*what is called 'high finance' is sometimes, if not frequently, deserving of the designation, 'low felony.'*" It is not necessary to practice highway robbery in order to be a thief. To purchase goods for less than their proper value because the seller cannot help himself, is just as much stealing as is selling them for more than they are worth because of misrepresentation.

On this point the Scriptures are very specific: "*A false balance is abomination to the LORD: but a just weight is His delight.*" Proverbs 11:1. "*Divers weights, and divers measures, both of them are alike abomination to the LORD.*" Proverbs 20:10. "*Thou shalt not have in thy bag divers weights, a great and a small. Thou shalt not have in thine house divers measures, a great and a small. But thou shalt have a perfect and just weight, a perfect and just measure shalt thou have: that thy days may be lengthened in the land which the LORD thy God giveth thee. For all that do such things, and all that do unrighteously, are an abomination unto the LORD thy God.*" Deuteronomy 25:13-16. "*Are there yet the treasurers of wickedness in the house of the wicked, and the scant measure that is abominable? Shall I count them pure with the wicked balances, and with the bag of deceitful weights?*" Micah 6:10, 11.

The wise man describes a very common practice among buyers

and sellers that constitutes a form of thievery. *"It is naught, it is naught, saith the buyer: but when he is gone his way, then he boasteth."* **Proverbs 20:14.** It is a common practice for buyers to depreciate the article or property in order to get the price as low as possible, and then boast of their business skill in driving a sharp bargain. This will not stand the searching test of honesty as set forth in the eighth commandment.

UNPAID DEBTS

The borrower never owns what he borrows, even though he keeps it for a long time. It is not his by mere possession. His obligation is a debt, and an unpaid debt is stealing. *"The wicked borroweth, and payeth not again."* **Psalms 37:21.** The person who borrows money or anything else without the expectation or ability to repay it is to all intents and purposes a thief. The same is true of the person who purchases or borrows with a good intent to repay, but refuses to do so when the debt is due. Many debts are contracted when it should be known that the promise to pay or repay can never be fulfilled, and this also comes within the category of stealing.

The person who has many unpaid bills and who is wasteful and extravagant in his own living is a thief of the worst sort. Borrowing or contracting debts that are never paid is too often a polite way of stealing.

The poet **Emerson** said:

"Wilt thou seal up the avenues of ill?
Pay every debt as if God wrote the bill."

And **Shakespeare** gave the following wise counsel:

"Neither a borrower nor a lender be:
For loan oft loses both itself and friend;
And borrowing dulls the edge of husbandry."

This form of stealing includes the borrowing of books that are never returned to the owner. **Disraeli** wrote in his *Curiosities of Literature*: *"Great collections of books are subject to certain accidents besides the damp, the worms, and the rats; one not less common is that*

117

of the borrowers, not to say a word of the purloiners." He must have had some of the experiences common to most of the owners of books.

THIEVES OF REPUTATION

Through vicious gossip or slander a person can be robbed of his good name or reputation, and this is the most damaging of all forms of thievery. A person's reputation is the capital stock on which he does business or makes a success in his work, and he is robbed of his usefulness in proportion to the injury done to his name. This is a form of stealing that never enriches the robber. It does injury to others without being in any way beneficial to the thief.

This principle is well stated by **Shakespeare:**

"Good name in man and woman, dear my lord,
Is the immediate jewel of their souls:
Who steals my purse steals trash;
But he that filches from me my good name
Robs me of that which not enriches him,
And makes me poor indeed."

It is worse still to plant doubts that will rob others of their religious hope and expectation, so that they lose eternal life. But in all forms of stealing, the thief himself is the chief victim and receives the greatest injury.

"Thieving, then, in its mildest forms, cheats the cheater. At best, it makes the one who practices it a parasite. That, in itself, is tragedy. No man can really get away with stealing. If no one else finds him out, his sin will. In fact, the most pathetic thief is the one who is getting away with his dishonesty. Sin is always a failure, but it never fails so disastrously as when it succeeds. It is always deadly, but it never kills so brutally as when it seems to give life."
–CLOVIS G. CHAPPELL, *Ten Rules for Living,* p. 128.

RESTITUTION

Obedience to the eighth commandment demands restitution of all that has been taken wrongfully and the paying of all debts and obligations to both God and man. Here is the law of restitution and its divine promise: *"If the wicked restore the pledge, give again that he had robbed, walk in the statutes of life, without committing iniquity; he shall surely live, he shall not die. None of his sins that he hath committed shall be mentioned unto him: he hath done that which is lawful and right; he shall surely live."* Ezekiel 33:15, 16.

When Zacchaeus found Jesus and salvation, He made full restitution for all his fraudulent dealings as a publican, or taxgatherer. *"Zacchaeus stood, and said unto the Lord; Behold, Lord, the half of my goods I give to the poor; and if I have taken anything from any man by false accusation, I restore him fourfold. And Jesus said unto him, This day is salvation come to this house, forsomuch as he also is a son of Abraham."* Luke 19:8, 9.

The inference of Jesus is that salvation will never come to the person who does not straighten up his financial affairs in harmony with the eighth commandment and Christian principles. All the sorrow and weeping over the sin of stealing that we are capable of will never atone for sins that ought to be confessed and made right by full restitution. Nor will unkept promises square the account in the books of heaven. Christians must be scrupulously honest in every respect. Then only can we expect the smile of God and the approval of heaven.

THE SIN OF
FALSE WITNESSING

11

"**T**hou shalt not bear false witness against thy neighbor." Exodus 20:16. The second table of the decalogue is summed up in the statement, *"Thou shalt love thy neighbor as thyself."* The ninth commandment forbids the bearing of any testimony by word or conduct that is contrary to that love for one's neighbor which the law demands. According to the parable of the good Samaritan, all our fellow men, including our enemies, are embraced in the term "neighbor." The sixth, seventh, and eighth commands have to do with man's life, virtue, and property. The ninth safeguards his reputation, which is of far more value than his external possessions.

The assassination of character is a more contemptible sin than the killing of the body or the stealing of property. Most of the other commands have to do with man's overt acts, or outward conduct, but the ninth deals with his words. So important is human speech that two out of the ten commandments regulate the use of the tongue. The third safeguards the name of God; the ninth, the name, or reputation, of men. It has been said that *"character is what you are; and reputation, what others think you are."* Therefore false witnessing can only harm one's reputation. It cannot injure the character. Others may injure the reputation, but the character can be marred only by the person himself. False testimony may injure one's standing with his neighbors, but it cannot alter his standing with God, who will eventually vindicate the good names of His own.

A GOOD NAME

The wise man said, *"A good name is rather to be chosen than great riches."* **Proverbs 22:1**. A good name is the most priceless possession a person has. It is worth more than all the gold and silver and wealth in the world. The man who attempts to rob another of his good name or to build up his own name on the ruins of another's reputation is a sinner of the worst type. But we must not fail to distinguish between character and reputation. Character is what we really are in the estimation of God. It is therefore in man's own keeping and no one can touch it except him. Every man can determine what his own character will be. But reputation is our neighbors' opinion of us and is therefore wholly in their keeping. Our reputations depend on what our neighbors think and say about us. In no respect are we more fully our brother's keeper than in regard to his reputation. When we injure his name by false witnessing, we betray a most sacred trust, for which we shall be called to account in the judgment.

DUTY OF WITNESSES

It is the duty of a witness to testify to the truth. A witness in court takes a solemn oath to tell *"the truth, the whole truth, and nothing but the truth,"* and the Christian standard for testifying out of court is just as high. The divine instruction is, *"Speak ye every man to his neighbor; execute the judgment of truth and peace in your gates."* **Zechariah 8:16**. In this respect as in all others Jesus is the supreme example. He is called *"the faithful Witness"* and *"the faithful and true Witness."* **Revelation 1:5; 3:14**. *"The truthful Witness"* is the Weymouth translation. To Pilate Jesus said, *"To this end was I born, and for this cause came I into the world, that I should bear witness unto the truth. Everyone that is of the truth heareth My voice."* **John 18:37**.

Jesus never minimized or exaggerated the truth in His witnessing. He never bore false testimony, nor did He stoop to the telling of those half truths that are sometimes the most dangerous of all lies. Of these **Tennyson** wrote:

> *"That a lie which is half a truth is ever the blackest of lies;*
> *That a lie which is all a lie may be met and fought with outright-*
> *But a lie that is part a truth is a harder matter to fight."*

Before bearing any witness concerning others we should be sure of the facts in the case and remember how often our own conduct has been misrepresented and misjudged because of partial evidence. "The whole truth" demands full knowledge without which it is impossible to be a faithful and true witness. Without that knowledge we have no right to speak.

THE SIN OF PERJURY

First of all, the ninth commandment forbids perjury in courts of justice. Perjury is the bearing of false witness while under oath to tell the truth. Although universally committed, it is considered a very serious crime. If justice is to be administered, the truth must be established by evidence which in turn must be established by the testimony of the witnesses. Justice can be based only on truth, and therefore, false testimony brings about a miscarriage of justice. For this reason perjury is made a criminal offense.

False testimony that defeats the ends of justice and robs one's neighbor of his possessions, his reputation, his liberty, or even his life, is the offense prohibited by the ninth commandment. This precept is broken by the judge who prostitutes his office by bribery, the lawyer who seeks to have the innocent condemned and the guilty set free, and the witness who deliberately distorts facts and invents lies to benefit friends or punish enemies. There is an old Dutch proverb which says, *"Give me a line of my neighbor's writing and I will hang him on the gallows."* This indicates the gross injustice that can be done by false testimony.

But whether the unfavorable decision is rendered by a judge or jury or a neighbor, because of false testimony, makes but little difference. The penalties imposed by the court of public opinion are often more severe and unjust than those executed by a court of law where evidence is more carefully sifted and examined. Christians should be at least as fair as courts claim to be in ruling that "a man is innocent until he is proved guilty," and the proof that condemns him must be "beyond a reasonable doubt." If Christians practiced this rule it would eliminate nine tenths of the gossip that is cursing the modern church.

THE SIN OF LYING

Lying is devilish. It is satanic. Of Satan it is said, *"He was a murderer from the beginning, and abode not in the truth, because there is no truth in him. When he speaketh a lie, he speaketh of his own: for he is a liar, and the father of it."* **John 8:44**. All lying therefore is devil inspired, and Jesus declared that liars are of their father, the devil. Many other texts indicate how abominable lying is in the estimation of the *"God of truth."*

"Lying lips are abomination to the LORD: but they that deal truly are His delight." **Proverbs 12:22**. *"A false witness shall not be unpunished, and he that speaketh lies shall not escape."* **Proverbs 19:5**. Among the six things the Lord especially hates are *"a lying tongue,... a heart that deviseth wicked imaginations, feet that be swift in running to mischief, a false witness that speaketh lies, and he that soweth discord among brethren."* **Proverbs 6:17-19**.

It has been said that *"a lie has no legs,"* because it is supported and carried by other lies. It is just as much a crime to circulate counterfeit money as to make it, and it is just as much a sin to circulate malicious lies as to manufacture them. A lie can be acted as well as spoken. Whatever is told as truth with the intent that it be accepted as truth but which is known to be false, or is deliberately placed in a false light or is exaggerated, with the intention of injuring the reputation of another, comes under the severest condemnation of the ninth commandment. We must make a distinction, of course, between unconscious falsehood based on misinformation or lack of knowledge and deliberate lying.

It is said that many thousands of people are color blind and that this enhances the danger of traffic accidents because they cannot distinguish the red lights from the green. This is also true in a spiritual sense. Many persons are always seeing things in a wrong light because they are spiritually color blind. We hear much about the innocence of "white lies," and although some lies may look white, and thus harmless to some persons who lie for their own convenience and profit, the fact is that all lies are as black as the bottomless pit whence they come. Our estimate of sin is largely determined by the spiritual condition of the heart. Everything looks green to those who look through green glasses and red to those who look through red glasses. With a heart and mind like Christ's we shall view sin with the same hatred as He does. It is said of Jesus that

He *"loved righteousness, and hated iniquity."* **Hebrews 1:9.**

It seems that lying is especially hateful to Him who is the Truth. Three times He declares in the last two chapters of the Book of books that *"all liars"* and **"whosoever loveth and maketh a lie"** will be excluded from the kingdom of glory and the celestial city, and will *"have their part in the lake which burneth with fire and brimstone: which is the second death."* **Revelation 21:8; 22:15.** This is the fate of liars, because false witnessing reveals the condition of the heart and character. Jesus declared that *"false witness"* comes *"out of the heart,"* and that *"out of the abundance of the heart the mouth speaketh,"* and therefore, *"every idle word that men shall speak, they shall give account thereof in the day of judgment. For by thy words thou shalt be justified, and by thy words thou shalt be condemned."* **Matthew 15:19; 12:34-37.** Truth always comes out of a true heart and falsehood out of a false heart, **"for the tree is known by his fruit."**

THE SIN OF SLANDER

The worst of all forms of false witnessing is slander, which is a falsehood deliberately invented and maliciously circulated. Slander appropriately has been called *"tongue murder."* The devil is the great slanderer, *"the accuser of the brethren."* *"Devil"* is the Greek name for "accuser" and "slanderer." Of the sin of slander **G. Campbell Morgan** says:

> *"Perhaps no form of injury done by man to men is more despicable than this. The person who makes use of it is one compared with whom the highwayman is a gentleman, and the assassin almost kind. The highwayman robs of material things that have been gained, and may be replaced. The assassin ends the life by swift or sudden stroke, often with little pain; but the slanderer who invents a lie, and uses it, forms a weapon which takes away a reputation, and all the chances are against its ever being regained; and thus oftentimes causes untold and prolonged suffering to the innocent, while, in the majority of cases, he himself goes undiscovered and unpunished."*
> *—The Ten Commandments,* pp. 101, 102.

Everywhere reputations are being murdered by vitriolic tongues and pens. *"He that hideth hatred with lying lips, and he that uttereth a slander, is a fool,"* declared the Lord through Solomon. (**Proverbs 10:18.**) Through David He said, *"Whoso privily slandereth his neighbor, him will I cut off."* **Psalms 101:5.** This sin is appropriately described in *Cyrnbeline*:

> *"'Tis slander,*
> *Whose edge is sharper than the sword, whose tongue*
> *Outvenoms all the worms of Nile, whose breath*
> *Rides on the posting winds and doth belie*
> *All corners of the world; kings, queens, and states,*
> *Maids, matrons, nay, the secrets of the grave*
> *This viperous slander enters."*

Talebearing is closely related to slander. *"Thou shalt not go up and down as a talebearer among thy people"* (**Leviticus 19:16**), is a divine application of the truth of the ninth commandment. The wise man said, *"A talebearer revealeth secrets: but he that is of a faithful spirit concealeth the matter." "The words of a talebearer are as wounds." "Where no wood is, there the fire goeth out: so where there is no talebearer, the strife ceaseth."* **Proverbs 11:13; 18:8; 26:20.** There are usually plenty of fire tenders to pile on the fuel.

Talebearing is the repeating of evil reports without ascertaining whether or not they are true. The circulation of any story that reflects on the reputation of another is a violation of the ninth commandment. Talebearing is one of the most common manifestations of false witnessing, and every Christian needs to pray daily and earnestly the petition of the psalmist, *"Set a watch, O LORD, before my mouth; keep the door of my lips."* **Psalms 141:3.**

> *"A whisper broke the air,*
> *A soft light tone, and low,*
> *Yet barbed with shame and woe;*
> *Now, might it only perish there,*
> *Nor further go!*
>
> *"Ah me! a quick and eager ear*
> *Caught up the little-meaning sound;*
> *Another voice has breathed it dear,*

And so it wandered round,
From ear to lip, from lip to ear,
Until it reached a gentle heart,
And that–it broke."

The peddler of malicious gossip is a false witness, but his testimony is harmless without a hearer. Just as the receiver of stolen goods is equally guilty with the thief, so the listener to falsehood is equally guilty with the gossiper. Someone has said that the tongues of busybodies are like the tails of Samson's foxes–they carry firebrands enough to set the world aflame. The psalmist said: *"Thy tongue deviseth mischiefs; like a sharp razor, working deceitfully." "They have sharpened their tongues like a serpent; adder's poison is under their lips."* Psalms 52:2; 140:3.

Just as the physician determines the state of physical health by looking at the tongue, so a spiritual physician can tell the condition of one's spiritual state by the use he makes of his tongue. It has been said that *"you can generally tell the metal of a bell by the sound of the clapper."* Just so you can tell the metal of a man by the sound of his words. The following is good advice for all of us:

"If wisdom's ways ye wisely seek,
Five things observe with care:
Of whom you speak, to whom you speak,
And how, and when, and where."

OTHER FORMS OF FALSE WITNESSING

False witnessing assumes many different forms. Even silence under some circumstances, when you know the slander to be false and do not speak in defense of the person defamed, is false witnessing. There are times when "silence is golden," and other times when it is lying.

"By holding our peace when we have it in our power to defend, by failing to mention the good when the evil is spoken of, by encouraging the telling of evil by eager listening, we assault the reputation of our neighbor by the assent of our silence."
–SCHENCK, *The Ten Commandments*, p. 127.

Suggestive hints and insinuating questions also constitute false witnessing. Satan's question, *"Doth Job fear God for naught?"* carried with it an implication of a sinister motive in his service that was far worse than a direct accusation. A person cannot be punished for asking a question, and yet it may have all the evil effect of a serious charge. A question in regard to a person's motives plants a seed of doubt that cannot be removed because it cannot be disproved. Faultfinding is another form of transgression. The person who seeks for faults in others will find them, for we usually find what we look for and often fail to see anything else. A vulture flies over a beautiful landscape and sees nothing except what it is looking for, a putrefying carcass. The many beautiful things are overlooked. The same is true of a faultfinder. The beauties of character are unseen, and the eyes are fixed on the little that is disagreeable and ugly.

Flattery is another form of false witnessing that imperils the souls of both the flatterer and the flattered. Flattery is always an exaggeration of the truth and is therefore a lie. A highly colored and overdrawn estimate of another defeats its own end. **Shakespeare** said, *"They do abuse the king that flatter him."* The Scriptures declare that *"a man that flattereth his neighbor spreadeth a net for his feet."* **Proverbs 29:5.** Of the flatterer we again read, *"The words of his mouth were smoother than butter, but war was in his heart: his words were softer than oil, yet were they drawn swords."* **Psalms 55:21.**

It has been said that *"flattery is soft soap, and soft soap is 90 per cent lye."*

"Greatly his foes he dreads, but more his friends,
He hurts me most who lavishly commends."
                      –CHURCHILL.

"'Tis an old maxim in the schools,
That flattery's the food of fools."
                    –SWIFT.

This form of false witness includes the untrue recommendations and testimonials of character and ability often given because of friendship or other obligations.

POWER OF THE TONGUE

The tongue is a mighty power for good or ill, and it should therefore be kept under careful control. *"Let every man be swift to hear, slow to speak"* is good counsel. (**James 1:19.**) Again we read, *"In the multitude of words there wanteth not sin: but he that refraineth his lips is wise."* **Proverbs 10:19.** *"Be not rash with thy mouth, and let not thine heart be hasty to utter anything before God: for God is in heaven, and thou upon earth: therefore let thy words be few."* **Ecclesiastes 5:2.**

It seems that the Scriptures contain more warnings against the transgression of the ninth commandment than of any of the other ten. The bearing of false witness is a universal sin. **Will Carleton** gives wise counsel in verse in regard to the use of the tongue:

"Boys flying kites haul in their white-winged birds;
You can't do that way when you're flying words.
'Careful with fire,' is good advice you know,
'Careful with words,' is ten times doubly so.
Thoughts unexpressed may sometimes fall back dead;
But God Himself can't kill them when they're said."

One writer has put together in verse the proverbs of different peoples and lands dealing with the power of the tongue either to heal or to wound:

"'The boneless tongue, so small and weak,
Can crush and kill,' declared the Greek.
'The tongue destroys a greater horde,'
The Turk asserts, 'than does the sword.'
The Persian proverb wisely saith,
'A lengthy tongue–an early death';
Or sometimes takes this form instead:
'Don't let your tongue cut off your head.'
'The tongue can speak a word whose speed,'
Says the Chinese, 'outstrips the steed.'
While Arab sage doth this impart:
'The tongue's great storehouse is the heart.'
From Hebrew hath the maxim sprung–
'Though feet should slip, ne'er let the tongue.'

The sacred writer crowns the whole:
'Who keeps his tongue doth keep his soul.'"

CONTROL OF THE TONGUE

"My brethren, be not many masters, knowing that we shall receive the greater condemnation. For in many things we offend all. If any man offend not in word, the same is a perfect man, and able also to bridle the whole body. Behold, we put bits in the horses' mouths, that they may obey us; and we turn about their whole body. Behold also the ships, which though they be so great, and are driven of fierce winds, yet are they turned about with a very small helm, whithersoever the governor listeth.

"Even so the tongue is a little member, and boasteth great things. Behold, how great a matter a little fire kindleth! And the tongue is a fire, a world of iniquity: so is the tongue among our members, that it defileth the whole body, and setteth on fire the course of nature; and it is set on fire of hell. For every kind of beasts, and of birds, and of serpents, and of things in the sea, is tamed, and hath been tamed of mankind: but the tongue can no man tame; it is an unruly evil, full of deadly poison. Therewith bless we God, even the Father; and therewith curse we men, which are made after the similitude of God. Out of the same mouth proceedeth blessing and cursing. My brethren, these things ought not so to be." James 3:1-10.

It is here stated that the control of the tongue is the secret or evidence of perfection. It is as the bridle to the horse and the rudder to the ship. It is said to be "*a fire,*" which put to a proper use is a great blessing, but when out of control is a desolating curse, "*a world of iniquity,*" "*a deadly poison.*" While no man can tame his tongue, there is a power that can bring it under control. The transforming power of the gospel can made the tongue our servant rather than our master.

Through science we learn that all sounds, including our words, set in motion waves of air which continue to undulate to the utmost confines of space. The effect of our words in a moral sense is similar. A whispered rumor of a scandal may keep moving and spreading and wounding and bruising and killing till the very end of the reign of sin. The cure for loose talk and malicious gossip is not the vow of perpetual silence taken by a class of monks and recluses. The Lord intends that we should use our tongues to bless our fellow men, and in fact they have no other use, with the exception of giving praise to God.

"Ye are My witnesses, saith the Lord, that I am God" (Isaiah 43:12), sets forth the chief testimony to be borne by man. (See also Matthew 28:19, 20; Acts 1:8.) That God's last-day witnesses will have complete control of their tongues is evident from several scriptures. *"The remnant of Israel shall not do iniquity, nor speak lies; neither shall a deceitful tongue be found in their mouth." "And in their mouth was found no guile: for they are without fault before the throne of God."* Zephaniah 3:13; Revelation 14:5.

"Thou shalt love thy neighbor as thyself" is the positive phase of the ninth commandment. *"Love worketh no ill to his neighbor: therefore love is the fulfilling of the law."* Romans 13:10. Love is the golden rule in practice. It is doing to others as we would have them do unto us, and speaking of others as we would have them speak of us.

> *"If you see a tall fellow ahead of the crowd,*
> *A leader of men, marching fearless and proud,*
> *And you know of a tale whose mere telling aloud*
> *Would cause his proud head in shame to be bowed,*
> *It's a pretty good plan to forget it."*

THE SIN OF COVETOUSNESS

12

"*T hou shalt not covet thy neighbor's house, thou shalt not covet thy neighbor's wife, nor his manservant, nor his maidservant, nor his ox, nor his ass, nor anything that is thy neighbor's.*" Exodus 20:17.

Covetousness implies a sense of delight in, and desire to possess, some object, especially by unjust and unlawful means. It is to set the heart on something belonging to another and to which one has no right without an adequate return for the value received. In an evil sense covetousness is inordinate desire or affection. In the New Testament it is often translated *"desire," "lust,"* and *"concupiscence."* It is a desire to possess what is not lawfully obtainable.

If the desired object can be obtained lawfully, it is not a sin to desire what we do not possess. It is wrong to covet when the thing desired is out of reach through legitimate means. It is a sin to want my neighbor's property to the extent that I would get it by almost any means. Covetousness is concentrated selfishness and is universally condemned throughout the Scriptures.

The other nine commandments have to do chiefly with the outward conduct–with overt acts. But the tenth reaches into the inner life and regulates the motives that give birth to deeds. The thoughts are the parents of the acts. This command may therefore be transgressed without the knowledge of others. It is the most heart searching of all the commands of the law. The thoughts and intents of the heart are the fountain from which words and deeds flow, and this last command goes back to the very source of sin. It prohibits the evil desire that gives birth to unlawful conduct.

The tenth commandment shows that when we set covetous eyes on what is not ours, it is as much a sin as the act of stealing itself. Our desires are actions in embryo. Even though the evil desires never reach the stage of conduct, they are in themselves sinful in the sight of God. The sinful inclination of the heart is a transgression of the law with the penalty of eternal death. Obedience to the decalogue must include the thoughts and motives as well as the words and deeds. These righteous precepts cannot be kept by any person who has a desire to break them.

> *"Trace every breach of the moral law, whether murder, adultery, theft, slander, or any of the sins of which these are the heads and representatives, back to their source, and it will be found that it has been suggested and inspired by one or another of the vices of which covetousness is the chief."*
> –JOHN BURR, *Studies on the Ten Commandments*, p. 146.

SUMMARY OF THE LAW

Since covetousness is the sin that leads to all other sins, the tenth commandment is a summary, not only of the second table of the decalogue, but of the whole law. The violation of this precept may lead to the transgression of every other. Covetousness is the fountain from which flow the poisonous streams of idolatry, hypocrisy, Sabbath desecration, disobedience to parents, murder, fornication, stealing, and lying or the bearing of false witness.

The apostle Paul connects the tenth with the first commandment in the following texts: *"Mortify therefore your members which are upon the earth; fornication, uncleanness, inordinate affection, evil concupiscence, and covetousness, which is idolatry."* Colossians 3:5. *"This ye know, that no whoremonger, nor unclean person, nor covetous man, who is an idolater, hath any inheritance in the kingdom of Christ and of God."* Ephesians 5:5.

Like the Bible itself, the decalogue ends where it begins, thus making a complete circle, the emblem of perfection. The law of God is complete, perfect, and eternal. It contains a depth and comprehensiveness that is immeasurable and includes every virtue within the range of human duty. It also strictly and directly prohibits every vice within reach of human conduct. It contains *"the whole duty of man."*

The tenth commandment is virtually repeated in **Deuteronomy 5:21**: *"Neither shalt thou desire thy neighbor's wife, neither shalt thou covet thy neighbor's house, his field, or his manservant, or his maidservant, his ox, or his ass, or anything that is thy neighbor's."* This shows that the law against coveting is a single precept and cannot be divided into two separate commands, as is done by the Roman Catholics and other religious bodies. Seven times in the tenth commandment we are reminded that the thing coveted belongs to another. After naming seven of man's possessions, for fear that something else might be found to covet, the all-inclusive statement is added, *"or anything that is thy neighbor's."*

David wrote, *"The wicked boasteth of his heart's desire, and blesseth the covetous, whom the LORD abhorreth."* Psalms 10:3.

The counsel of Jethro to Moses in the wilderness contained this statement: *"Moreover thou shalt provide out of all the people able men, such as fear God, men of truth, hating covetousness; and place such over them, to be rulers of thousands, and rulers of hundreds, rulers of fifties, and rulers of tens: and let them judge the people at all seasons."* Exodus 18:21,22. Hatred of covetousness is an important qualification for leadership in God's work. The following divine woe is pronounced upon the covetous: *"Woe to them that devise iniquity, and work evil upon their beds! when the morning is light, they practice it, because it is in the power of their hand. And they covet fields, and take them by violence; and houses, and take them away: so they oppress a man and his house, even a man and his heritage."* Micah 2:1, 2.

No student of the New Testament can claim that the tenth commandment came to an end at the cross or has been supplanted by grace. *"Take heed, and beware of covetousness: for a man's life consisteth not in the abundance of the things which he possesseth,"* is the message of Christ, enforced by a parable. (Luke 12:13-23.) Paul wrote, *"Be not deceived: neither fornicators, nor idolaters, nor adulterers, nor effeminate, nor abusers of themselves with mankind, nor thieves, nor covetous, nor drunkards, nor revilers, nor extortioners, shall inherit the kingdom of God."* 1 Corinthians 6: 9, 10. This is almost a complete summary of the law. In this text the covetous are placed in the midst of the worst of sinners and criminals.

In **1 Thessalonians 2:5** is a warning against wearing *"a cloak of covetousness."* Such a cloak is usually called keen business foresight and ability to get ahead by outwitting and outmaneuvering others, but God calls it hypocrisy. After making the statement, *"Beware ye of the leaven of the Pharisees, which is hypocrisy,"* Jesus emphasized His meaning by saying, *"Take heed, and beware of covetousness."* **Luke 12:1, 15.** The cloak of hypocrisy worn by the Pharisees was really a *"cloak of covetousness."*

The height of the Christian standard is set forth in the following texts: *"But fornication, and all uncleanness, or covetousness, let it not be once named among you, as becometh saints." "Let your conversation be without covetousness; and be content with such things as ye have: for He hath said, I will never leave thee, nor forsake thee."* **Ephesians 5:3; Hebrews 13:5.** There is a great deal of covetous conversation even among professed Christians. Great care should be exercised in speaking of our desires for what others possess lest it lead to covetousness.

INSATIABLE DESIRE

Covetousness is never satisfied. The passion of covetousness grows till it completely possesses a man and corrupts his character. *"Send us gold, for we Spaniards have a disease which can only be cured by gold,"* is the reported message of **Cortez** to Montezuma, the ruler of Mexico. The spirit of covetousness is set forth in **Ecclesiastes 5:10-13:** *"He that loveth silver shall not be satisfied with silver; nor he that loveth abundance with increase: this also is vanity. When goods increase, they are increased that eat them: and what good is there to the owners thereof, saving the beholding of them with their eyes? The sleep of a laboring man is sweet, whether he eat little or much: but the abundance of the rich will not suffer him to sleep. There is a sore evil which I have seen under the sun, namely, riches kept for the owners thereof to their hurt."* (See also **Psalms 49:6-20.**)

To satisfy a covetous man with gold and property would be like trying to satisfy a fire with fuel. The more wood you feed the flames, the more greedily the fire burns, and the more a covetous person obtains, the more fiercely burns the flaming passion of avarice. Covetousness is ever eating and never full; it is ever lusting and never satisfied; it is ever getting and never giving. The poet **Rossetti** states it thus:

"Oh, what is earth, that we should build
Our houses here, and seek concealed
Poor treasure, and add field to field,
And heap to heap, and store to store,
Still grasping more, and seeking more,
While, step by step, Death nears the door!"

ROOT OF ALL EVIL

The apostle Paul said: *"The love of money is the root of all evil: which while some coveted after, they have erred from the faith, and pierced themselves through with many sorrows. But thou, O man of God, flee these things; and follow after righteousness, godliness, faith, love, patience, meekness."* 1 Timothy 6:10, 11. *"A root of all kinds of evil,"* is the rendering in the Revised Version. This is equivalent to saying that covetousness is the root of all evil. We have already found that covetousness leads to the transgression of all the commands of the decalogue.

In the Chinese language the word for covetousness is composed of three characters representing a woman between two trees. The covetousness of Eve in turning away from the tree of life to the forbidden fruit opened the door for the entrance of all the evils that have cursed this world under the reign of sin. Covetousness is the root cause of all crime. It is closely related to envy. In fact they are twin sisters. *"Wrath is cruel, and anger is outrageous; but who is able to stand before envy?"* is the question of the wise man.

It has been said that desire is *"action in the egg."* D. L. Moody quotes the following statement:

"The covetous person is a thief in the shell. The thief is a covetous person out of the shell. Let a covetous person see something that he desires very much; let an opportunity of taking it be offered; how very soon he will break through the shell and come out in his true character as a thief."
—Weighed and Wanting, p. 108.

The same can be said of all the other commands. The apostle Paul felt that he was living in harmony with the law till he beheld the tenth commandment under spiritual illumination, and then he considered himself a violator of the whole law and a slave to sin. (See **Romans 7:7, 14, 24, 25**.)

135

SCRIPTURAL EXAMPLES

The seriousness of the sin of coveting is illustrated by many examples in the Bible. Coveting the wisdom and experience of gods led Eve to steal the forbidden fruit and was the sin which brought all other sins in its train. Lot coveted the rich plains of Sodom, and when the city was destroyed he lost all his wealth and most of his family. Achan's covetousness made him a thief and resulted in his death and the defeat of all Israel. Here is his confession: *"Indeed I have sinned against the LORD God of Israel, and thus and thus have I done: When I saw among the spoils a goodly Babylonish garment, and two hundred shekels of silver, and a wedge of gold of fifty shekels weight, then I coveted them, and took them; and, behold, they are hid in the earth in the midst of my tent, and the silver under it."* Joshua 7:20, 21.

Gehazi was ruined by covetousness which led to deceit and lying. From Naaman he got more than he asked for, including his leprosy. He also received what was far worse–the disfavor of the prophet and the frown of God. David coveted the wife of Uriah, and in order to get what he unlawfully desired he committed both adultery and murder, and brought an everlasting reproach upon his own name and the cause of God. Ahab coveted the vineyard of Naboth, and his evil desire ended in murder, in order to obtain what he wanted. Balaam's covetous spirit turned him into an enemy of God and His people. He sold his prophetic birthright for the promised wealth of Balak, and he died in his sins.

Covetousness was the sin of Ananias and Sapphira, who selfishly tried to retain part of their pledge, and lost everything in untimely deaths. It was the sin of Simon who coveted and sought to purchase what money cannot buy, and of Judas who committed the crime of all crimes for the paltry sum of thirty pieces of silver, or about sixteen dollars, the price of a slave. From the gates of Eden to our own day we can trace the slimy trail of the serpent of covetousness, and he was never more active than at the present time of abounding selfishness.

LAWFUL COVETOUSNESS

But there is a form of desire, or covetousness, that is not only lawful, but is positively enjoined in the Scriptures. There are certain things that the Lord wants us to desire earnestly to the extent that we seek with all our hearts to obtain them. After describing the gifts of the Spirit, Paul said, *"But covet earnestly the best gifts: and yet show I unto you a more excellent way."* 1 Corinthians 12:31. The *"more excellent way"* is set forth in the next chapter, and is coveting after the spirit of love, which is of more value than all the gifts combined and without which they are useless. Every Christian should be able to say,

> *"If it be sin to covet love,*
> *I am the most offending soul alive."*

It is also lawful to earnestly covet knowledge, and then seek diligently to obtain it. It is always right to desire to be and do our very best. *"Blessed are they which do hunger and thirst after righteousness,"* is a divine approval on the right kind of covetousness. All depends on the objects desired and the right we have to possess them, or whether or not our neighbor desires us to possess what he has a right to convey for its equivalent in value. The right kind of coveting never deprives others of their possessions. Obtaining knowledge from others does not deplete their store, but rather increases and enriches the supply.

Those who seek the invisible and eternal things of character and spiritual values will be delivered from the sin of covetousness in its application to mere things. The covetousness of the psalmist was not sin when he said, *"One thing have I desired of the LORD, that will I seek after; that I may dwell in the house of the LORD all the days of my life, to behold the beauty of the LORD, and to enquire in His temple."* Psalms 27:4. We all need more of this kind of coveting.

Again the psalmist said: *"As the hart panteth after the water brooks, so panteth my soul after Thee, O God."* *"My soul longeth, yea, even fainteth for the courts of the LORD: my heart and my flesh crieth out for the living God."* Psalms 42:1; 84:2. After naming the things that wicked men covet, Jesus summed up all lawful desires in the statement: *"But seek ye first the kingdom of God, and His righteousness; and all these things shall be added unto you."* Matthew 6:33.

It is not difficult to distinguish between right and wrong kinds of coveting. The tenth commandment forbids the coveting of material possessions, because if obtained the owner is deprived of them. This is not true of intellectual and spiritual possessions. He who covets wisdom and knowledge or any of the gifts and fruits of the Spirit, and through effort obtains them, does not rob any other person of them. In fact lawful coveting enriches both the giver and receiver, whereas unlawful covetousness impoverishes them both- one in material possessions and the other in spiritual possessions.

THE SPIRIT OF CONTENTMENT

The opposite of the avaricious and covetous spirit, which nothing can satisfy, is godly contentment, which can be known only by genuine Christians. Paul warns against those who suppose *"that gain is godliness,"* and then says: *"But godliness with contentment is great gain. For we brought nothing into this world, and it is certain we can carry nothing out. And having food and raiment let us be therewith content. But they that will be rich fall into temptation and a snare, and into many foolish and hurtful lusts, which drown men in destruction and perdition."* 1 Timothy 6:6-9.

Everything works together for the good of the godly who are content with whatever the Lord in His providence sends them. Paul also said, *"I have learned, in whatever state I am, therewith to be content."* Philippians 4:11. The author of the Hebrews said, *"Let your conversation be without covetousness; and be content with such things as ye have: for He hath said, I will never leave thee, nor forsake thee."* Hebrews 13:5. Covetousness is the great enemy of contentment, because it fixes our attention on what we have not rather than on what we have. It makes its victims unhappy and discontented. It makes men and women miserable instead of peaceful and contented.

DANGEROUS CONTENTMENT

But there is a dangerous contentment that must be avoided. It is the contentment and self-satisfaction of the Laodiceans: *"Unto the angel of the church of the Laodiceans write: These things saith the Amen, the faithful and true Witness, the beginning of the creation of God: I know thy works, that thou art neither cold nor hot: I would thou wert cold or hot. So then because thou art lukewarm, and neither cold nor hot, I will spue thee out of My mouth. Because thou sayest, I am rich, and increased with goods, and have need of nothing; and knowest not that thou art wretched, and miserable, and poor, and blind, and naked: I counsel thee to buy of Me gold tried in the fire, that thou mayest be rich; and white raiment, that thou mayest be clothed, and that the shame of thy nakedness do not appear; and anoint thine eyes with eyesalve, that thou mayest see."* Revelation 3:14-18.

We must never be content with ourselves or our attainments in knowledge, or spiritual experience. Such contentment always leads to spiritual stagnation and death. Paul was satisfied with his Master, and he found contentment in his work. He was also contented with his temporal blessings. But godly contentment never places a premium on indolence. It does not destroy lawful ambition and aggressiveness. It does not produce a listless, lazy attitude that makes no effort to improve conditions. It increases one's desire for more knowledge, deeper piety, and a richer spiritual experience. The more one obtains in spiritual experience and blessings, the more he desires. While that which is obtained is wonderfully satisfying, the cry of the heart is:

"More about Jesus I would know,
More of His grace to others show;
More of His saving fullness see,
More of His love who died for me."

Godly contentment comes only to those who do their very best and then believe that *"all things work together for good to them that love God, to them who are the called according to His purpose."* Romans 8:28. Only those who love their neighbors as themselves and who practice the golden rule can obey the tenth commandment. No one ever covets the possessions of talents or the acquirements of those he really loves. A real mother does not covet the beauty of her daughter, or a father the education and talents of his son. How true it is that *"he that loveth another hath fulfilled the law."* Therefore *"let us love one another: for love is of God."* Covetousness feeds on selfishness. It cannot exist where love rules and abounds. *"Love is the fulfilling of the law."*

THE NEW COMMANDMENT

13

"A new commandment I give unto you, That ye love one another; as I have loved you, that ye also love one another. By this shall all men know that ye are My disciples, if ye have love one to another." "This is My commandment, That ye love one another, as I have loved you. Greater love hath no man than this, that a man lay down his life for his friends. Ye are My friends, if ye do whatsoever I command you." John 13:34, 35; 15:12-14.**

This "new commandment" is sometimes called the eleventh commandment, and yet it is very evident that it adds nothing to the ten. Its purpose is to show that love is the very essence of the law and the motive power of obedience. The new commandment is the sum and substance of the whole law. To love with the same unselfish and devoted fervor with which Christ loved, sums up all Christian living. The measure of Christian love, declared Jesus, is to love one another, *"even as I have loved you."* (Revised Version.) Jesus declared that the greatest evidence of mere human love is for a man to lay down his life for his friends, but that is not enough to satisfy the demands of the law of love. Christ's love was still greater, for He laid down His life for His enemies, and this is the measure of love set forth in the new commandment. Someone has said that *"self-sacrifice is the high-water mark of love."*

EVIDENCE OF DISCIPLESHIP

Jesus said that the exhibition of a love like His is the evidence to "all men" that we are His disciples. Not by the wearing of some particular garb or by subscribing to a certain set of doctrines or even by maintaining membership in a certain church, is discipleship determined, but by love in action. Love is the badge of Christianity. **Tertullian** said, *"The working of such love puts a brand upon us; for see, say the heathen, how they love each other."* This was the sign by which the heathen recognized the early Christians. It was a far more important evidence than their profession.

But genuine love always produces obedience. Obedience therefore is the evidence of love. *"Ye are my friends, if ye do whatsoever I command you,"* said Jesus. (John 15:14.) Again He said: *"If ye love Me, keep My commandments." "He that hath My commandments, and keepeth them, he it is that loveth Me: and he that loveth Me shall be loved of My Father, and I will love him, and will manifest Myself to him.... If a man love Me, he will keep My words: and My Father will love him, and we will come unto him and make our abode with him. He that loveth Me not keepeth not My sayings."* John 14:15, 21-24.

This principle was also set forth by the apostles. *"This is the love of God, that we keep His commandments: and His commandments are not grievous."* 1 John 3:3. God defines love as obedience, because it always leads to obedience. The apostle Paul said, *"Owe no man anything, but to love one another: for he that loveth another hath fulfilled the law.... Love worketh no ill to his neighbor: therefore love is the fulfilling of the law."* Romans 13:8-10.

The obedience of love is never grievous, burdensome, or sacrificial. Love knows no sacrifice or hardship. Christianity is not a religion of pious emotions, but of practical godliness.

"God requires a great deal more of a holy person than rolling in the dirt, speaking in tongues, and shouting.... Much that is called holiness is passing through sentimental hallucinations."
–J. B. ROUNDS, *The Ten Commandments for Today,* p. 17.

An emotional religion may arouse the feelings and produce some tears, but the effect is something like that of the summer sun on a snow-covered iceberg-nothing but surface slush. Practical godliness has more permanent results. "Keep on loving" and "keep on doing" is the meaning of our texts in the original. The demand is for a permanent spiritual experience and not spasmodic love and obedience.

NOT A NEW LAW

Jesus did not say that He was giving a new law to supplant the old. His teaching and practice in no way minimized the value and force of the decalogue. He indignantly denied that His advent in any way affected the perpetuity and binding claims of the law: *"Do not for a moment suppose that I have come to abrogate the law or the prophets: I have not come to abrogate them but to give them their completion. Solemnly I tell you that until heaven and earth pass away, not one iota or smallest detail will pass away from the law until all has taken place. Whoever therefore breaks one of these least commandments and teaches others to break them, will be called the least in the kingdom of the heavens; but whoever practices them and teaches them, he will be acknowledged as great in the kingdom of the heavens. For I assure you that unless your righteousness greatly surpasses that of the scribes and Pharisees, you will certainly not find entrance into the kingdom of the heavens."* Matthew 5:17-20, Weymouth translation.

How can a person read this statement and continue to believe and teach that Jesus abrogated the ten commandment law? In His life and teachings Jesus fulfilled the law in both its letter and its spirit. He could not do otherwise, for it is the summary of all truth, the standard of all righteousness, and the rule of the final judgment. Obedience to it is the test of discipleship and the evidence of love. In the light of Christ's emphatic statement, who dares say that the law of love was supplanted by grace? Grace thunders as loudly and insistently against sin as does law. Grace is the divine remedy for the disease of sin that is defined or revealed or diagnosed by law, and therefore one is ineffectual without the other. The very purpose of the gospel is to bring men and women into harmony with the law of God, which is the very foundation of His government. Therefore the person who violates even what he considers to be the least of the ten commandments is considered little or small by the inhabitants of heaven, and those who observe and teach them all are considered great.

It is bad enough to break one of these divine principles, but it is still worse to teach others to transgress. He who does this, as many religious leaders do, is indeed a little man engaged in a little business, and he will receive his just punishment.

A DIVINE COMMENT

Fortunately we have been given a divinely inspired comment on Christ's statement in regard to "a new commandment," so that there need be no confusion or misunderstanding as to His meaning: *"Brethren, I write no new commandment unto you, but an old commandment which ye had from the beginning. The old commandment is the word which ye have heard from the beginning. Again, a new commandment I write unto you, which thing is true in Him and in you: because the darkness is past, and the true light now shineth." "For this is the message that ye heard from the beginning, that we should love one another." "And now I beseech thee, lady, not as though I wrote a new commandment unto thee, but that which we had from the beginning, that we love one another. And this is love, that we walk after His commandments. This is the commandment, That, as ye have heard from the beginning, ye should walk in it."* 1 John 2:7, 8; 3:11; 2 John 5, 6.

These texts show clearly that the new commandment does not take the place of the old law, but it is the old law itself in a new setting. Love is as old as the human race and so is obedience to the law. But as the result of the advent of the Son of God and His demonstration of divine love on the cross, love is placed in a new and fresh light. It is new because of the new light thrown on the spiritual import of the law by the life, teachings, and death of Christ. Such love and obedience as were seen in Christ had never before been manifested.

Jesus came into the world to *"magnify the law, and make it honorable."* It was shown to be the law of love, and not a mere code of restrictions. Since Calvary, the decalogue has taken on a new meaning and significance and is seen in a new light. It has become *"so exceeding broad"* as to embrace not only the outward acts but also the inner motives and emotions. The command to love God and man is as old as the law itself. In fact, love was made the summary of the law at the time the law was given from Sinai. *"Hear, O Israel: The LORD our God is one LORD: and thou shalt love the LORD thy God with all thine heart, and with all thy soul, and with all thy might."* Deuteronomy 6: 4, 5. *"Thou shalt not avenge, nor bear any grudge against the children of thy people, but thou shalt love thy neighbor as thyself: I am the LORD."* Leviticus 19:18.

143

But while mankind had *"from the beginning"* the command to love God supremely and his neighbor as himself, the practice of this law of love as demonstrated in the life of Christ was new. It was old in age and teaching, but new in practice. It is ever fresh and new in the experience of every person who has been born again and on the fleshy tables of whose heart the law of God has been rewritten by the Holy Spirit in the living reality of the indwelling Christ. The decalogue thus becomes a new code of morals to those who through the new birth become new creatures and come under the dominion of the new covenant. To such a person *"all things are become new,"* even the law of ten commandments.

John declares that the commandment is new, *"because the darkness is passing away, and the true light already shineth."* (Revised Version.) We are told that Jesus is *"the true Light, which lighteth every man that cometh into the world."* **John 1:9.** His coming into the world in the likeness of sinful human flesh and living a life of perfect obedience, greatly magnified and illuminated the law. In fact, Christ is the living law. The decalogue was written in His heart, and He delighted to obey its precepts. He said, *"I delight to do Thy will, O My God: yea Thy law is within My heart."* **Psalms 40:8.**

The perfection of the decalogue, in comparison with all other laws, gives evidence of its divine origin, and the perfection of the life of Christ, in comparison with all other lives, gives evidence that He is divine. The same perfection and obedience in the lives of His disciples show that they have become *"partakers of the divine nature."* The law in its new setting constrains us to love all our neighbors, including our enemies, and thus follow in the footsteps of Him who loves us, even when we are His enemies. The law is new only in those who have been re-created, because the darkness is passing away before the true light that is shining into their hearts. It is the new love that makes the old commandments a new law.

LOVE FULFILLS THE LAW

"Owe nothing to anyone except mutual love; for he who loves his fellow man has satisfied the demands of the law. . . . Love avoids doing any wrong to one's fellow man, and is therefore complete obedience to law." **Romans 13:8-10,** Weymouth translation.

In these statements the apostle is speaking only of the second table of the law, which deals with human relations. But the same

144

principle applies to the first table, which regulates our duties to God. The duties and relationships of husband and wife to each other as set forth in the law of marriage are completely fulfilled in mutual love. Love meets all the demands of the law of marriage. Likewise love meets all the demands of the decalogue.

D. L. Moody quotes someone as saying:

> *"Love to God will admit no other god. Love resents everything that debases its object by representing it by an image. Love to God will never dishonor His name. Love to God will reverence His day. Love to parents makes one honor them. Hate, not love, is a murderer. Lust, not love, commits adultery. Love will give, but never steal. Love will not slander or lie. Love's eye is not covetous."*
> **–Weighed and Wanting,** pp. 124, 125.

The law is so completely fulfilled and summed up in love that "in heaven it is never heard of and never broken." Another has said:

> *"But in heaven,' service is not rendered in the spirit of legality. When Satan rebelled against the law of Jehovah, the thought that there was a law came to the angels almost as an awakening to something unthought of. In their ministry the angels are not as servants, but as sons. There is perfect unity between them and their Creator. Obedience is to them no drudgery. Love for God makes their service a joy."*
> **–E. G. WHITE,**
> **Thoughts From the Mount of Blessing,** p. 161.

While the Christian still loves the law of God in its material form, and his soul finds delight and sweetness in meditating on its righteous precepts, through increasing love he does *"by nature the things contained in the law,"* so that it is fulfilled without continuous, conscious thought or effort. It is not necessary for a husband and wife who dearly love each other to constantly study written rules of marriage conduct. When the law of love is written in the heart, its demands are met almost unconsciously.

The principle of love-obedience is beautifully set forth in the following statement:

145

"All true obedience comes from the heart. It was heart work with Christ. And if we consent, He will so identify Himself with our thoughts and aims, so blend our hearts and minds into conformity to His will, that when obeying Him we shall be but carrying out our own impulses. The will, refined and sanctified, will find its highest delight in doing His service. When we know God as it is our privilege to know Him, our life will be a life of continual obedience. Through an appreciation of the character of Christ, through communion with God, sin will become hateful to us."

–E. G. WHITE, *The Desire of Ages.* p. 668.

The same author again says:

"There are those who profess to serve God, while they rely upon their own efforts to obey His law, to form a right character, and secure salvation. Their hearts are not moved by any deep sense of the love of Christ, but they seek to perform the duties of the Christian life as that which God requires of them in order to gain heaven. Such religion is worth nothing. When Christ dwells in the heart, the soul will be so filled with His love, with the joy of communion with Him, that it will cleave to Him; and in the contemplation of Him, self will be forgotten. Love to Christ will be the spring of action. Those who feel the constraining love of God, do not ask how little may be given to meet the requirements of God; they do not ask for the lowest standard, but aim at perfect conformity to the will of their Redeemer. With earnest desire they yield all, and manifest an interest proportionate to the value of the object which they seek. A profession of Christ without this deep love, is mere talk, dry formality, and heavy drudgery."

–*Steps to Christ* (pocket edition), pp. 44, 45.

In our relations with both God and man nothing really counts except it be motivated by love. In the estimation of Christ the widow's love-gift of two mites, or two tenths of a cent, was greater than all the gifts of the wealthy combined. They all gave money, but the others gave little or nothing else. The widow gave love with her offering, and this is what made her offering great. She gave *"more than they all,"* was the verdict of Christ. No offering or service is acceptable to God unless it is impelled by love. God estimates value not by the greatness of the work done but by the love that motivates

146

the acts. When love is lacking the mere round of ceremony is an offense to Him.

THE MEASURE OF LOVE

In his letter to the Ephesian church Paul expressed His desire *"that Christ may dwell in your hearts by faith; that ye, being rooted and grounded in love, may be able to comprehend with all saints what is the breadth, and length, and depth, and height; and to know the love of Christ, which passeth knowledge, that ye might be filled with all the fullness of God."* Ephesians 3:17-19.

Because the cross alone measures *"the breadth, and length, and depth, and height"* of the love of God, it is beyond the comprehension of man. The love of Christ *"passeth knowledge."* Its *"breadth"* is wide enough to comprehend the whole world, including all races. Its *"length"* reaches down through all the ages from the beginning to the end of the reign of sin. Its *"depth"* reaches down to the lowest deeps of man's degradation and saves even *"unto the uttermost."* Its *"height"* includes the highest heaven to which it will eventually lift those who know its power.

Genuine love exceeds the righteousness of the scribes and Pharisees. It goes far beyond the letter of the law. It sacrifices without any thought of the cost, as was demonstrated by Mary Magdalene in the gift of the costly ointment devoted to Jesus at the feast. Love goes beyond the second mile in service. Only perfect love can fulfill a perfect law that is the very essence of love. Christ was love incarnate. All His words and acts were impelled by the motive of love. On the cross love atoned for the transgressions of the loveless. *"Sin is the transgression of the law and demands atonement. Love is the fulfilling of the law and provides atonement,"* said **G. Campbell Morgan**. *"The love of Christ constraineth us,"* was the maxim that revealed the impelling power that sent forth the early Christians to the spiritual conquest of the world.

EVIDENCE OF PERFECTION

Love and obedience after the order of Christ are the evidence of perfection. Jesus said: *"Ye have heard that it hath been said, Thou shalt love thy neighbor, and hate thine enemy. But I say unto you,*

Love your enemies, bless them that curse you, do good to them that hate you, and pray for them which despitefully use you, and persecute you; that ye may be the children of your Father which is in heaven: for He maketh His sun to rise on the evil and on the good, and sendeth rain on the just and on the unjust. For if ye love them which love you, what reward have ye? do not even the publicans the same? And if ye salute your brethren only, what do ye more than others? do not even the publicans so? Be ye therefore perfect, even as your Father which is in heaven is perfect." Matthew 5: 43-48.

The sermon on the mount was an exposition and interpretation of the moral law. It was the law as magnified by Christ under the spiritual illumination of His life and teachings. *"Hate thine enemy,"* is not a part of **Leviticus 19:18** or of any other scripture. It is not even in the Talmud. It was an inference drawn from the attitude of the Jewish leaders toward all other peoples whom they looked upon as enemies worthy only to be despised. The Romans had reasons for their charge that the Jews were haters of the whole human race. The Jews looked upon all Gentiles as dogs unworthy of the favor of God or man.

In the text just quoted the contrast between love and hate is set forth in four manifestations. The genuine Christian gives love in return for hate, kind words for curses, good deeds for evil treatment, and prayer for persecution. Because this is the way the Lord treats His enemies the same conduct in us becomes the evidence of our relationship to Him. Jesus declared that mere love exchanged for love is so human that even the heathen practice it. It therefore has no special virtue or value. In His attitude toward His enemies Christ demonstrated the superior kind of love, which is the sign of perfection in His followers. When we treat our enemies as God does, we shall be perfect, even as He is perfect. Love is the secret of godliness and perfection. This is what Christ meant when He said, *"Be ye therefore perfect, even as your Father which is in heaven is perfect."* **Matthew 5:48.** Christlike love and conduct is the answer to the meaning of this difficult text.

SUMMARY OF THE LAW

Jesus made it plain that love is the very summary of the law and therefore of the Scriptures: *"One of them, which was a lawyer, asked Him a question, tempting Him, and saying, Master, which is the great commandment in the law? Jesus said unto him, Thou shalt love the Lord thy God with all thy heart, and with all thy soul, and with all thy mind. This is the first and great commandment. And the second is like unto it, Thou shalt love thy neighbor as thyself. On these two commandments hang all the law and the prophets.*" Matthew 22:35-40. (See also **Mark 12:28-31.**)

The relative value of the commandments was a debated question among the scribes and Pharisees. They taught that there were 248 affirmative precepts, or as many as there are members of the human body, and 365 negative precepts, or as many as there are days in the year. This made a total of 613, the number of the letters in the decalogue. These precepts were carefully classified and weighed according to rabbinic estimation of their importance. The relative value of these various precepts was one of the greatest questions for dispute among the Jewish leaders, especially the scribes, who were the expounders of the law. For centuries this had been a favorite battleground of the lawyers and had divided the Jewish theologians into rival schools. They now attempted to involve Jesus in their controversy, not so much for the sake of information, but to test or tempt Him.

"Which is the chief of all the commands of the law?" (Weymouth) was the cunning question of the lawyer. Which is the first in rank and importance? Jesus answered His tempter by quoting Scripture, which was always His weapon of defense. After quoting **Deuteronomy 6:5**, and **Leviticus 19:18**, Jesus declared that *"the whole of the law and the prophets is summed up in these two commandments"* (Weymouth), or, *"on these two commandments hang all the law and the prophets."* In the statement, *"There is none other commandment greater than these,"* Jesus placed the two tables of the decalogue on an equal footing. He placed love for God first, because that is the absolute prerequisite of love for our fellow men. No person can love his neighbor as himself until he first loves God with all his heart, soul, mind, and strength. No person can be crooked in his dealings with his neighbor and straight with God at the same time. The two tables constitute one law, which is fulfilled by love. Every transgression of the law is a violation of love.

One writer has appropriately said:

"The ten commandments are each separately a gem of law for every carnal age, but the ten are truly only one, so that he who

149

*offends in one is guilty of all. To reduce the five books of law to the tables of the ten commandments is a task only God could perform. To avoid error in transcription, God wrote the law Himself on tables of stone (**Exodus 31:18; 24:12; 32:19; 34:1**). But the five books reduced to these ten commands were further reduced by Jesus to two (**Matt. 22:40**); and by Paul to one (**Rom. 13:10; Gal. 5:14**)."*
–J. B. ROUND, *The Ten Commandments for Today,* p. 149.

In its ultimate summary and abridgement the law is comprehended in the one word, LOVE.

Love is therefore the abridged edition of the law, just as the law is the abridged edition of the Scriptures. All the revelations of God to man are comprehended in love. Those who love God supremely will worship Him only, speak His name reverently, and observe His holy Sabbath. They will love their neighbors as themselves by honoring their parents and refraining from murder, fornication, theft, false witnessing, and covetousness. The law in the setting of love is beautifully described by a noted Bible student as follows:

"If man love God in all the breadth and beauty suggested by the words 'with all thy heart, and with all thy soul, and with all thy mind,' he cannot possibly find room for another God, and so the first word is kept. If man love God supremely, he will not suffer anything to stand between him and God, thus the graven image is broken to pieces, and swept away by the force of a stronger affection. Out of love will spring that hallowing of the name of God which will dry the springs of blasphemy, and make the double dealing of the hypocrite an impossibility. The Sabbath will be eagerly welcomed, and all its privileges earnestly and gladly appropriated when it is a season in which love may find its way into the attitude of worship, and the acts of service following therefrom.

"Passing to the second table, and looking now at love in its working toward others, it will at once be seen that the only sufficient power for obedience and honor rendered to parents is that of love. There will be no thought of murder until the awful moment has arrived in which the flame of love has died out upon the altar. Unchastity of every description is love's sure destruction, growing gross upon the very death of that which it so vilely personates. All theft is rendered impossible by true love for

one's neighbor. Love sits as a sentinel at the portal of the lips, and arrests the faintest whisper of false witness against a neighbor; nay, rather dwells within the heart, and slays the thought that might have inspired the whisper. It is love and love alone that, finding satisfaction in God, satisfies the heart's hunger, and prevents all coveting."

–G. CAMPBELL MORGAN,
The Ten Commandments, pp. 120, 121.

THE DEMANDS OF LOVE

The decalogue as interpreted by the new commandment demands that God be loved and served with all the emotions and affections of the heart, all the spiritual faculties of the soul, all the thinking powers of the intellect, and all the energies, might, and strength of the physical body. Nowhere in the Scriptures is God pictured as a stern and relentless executor of justice, unmingled with mercy. When the law is seen in its proper light it reveals the love of God as verily as does the cross of Calvary.

Only a supreme love for God can prevent idolatry, and since love must center in a person, it refuses to tolerate an image substitute which is not capable of loving or being loved. This inward affection will prevent all outward irreverence and hypocrisy. Sabbathkeeping without love becomes formal and spiritless and therefore a dreaded drudgery instead of anticipated delight. Love will produce respect and honor for parents whom God has appointed as guardians of His heritage, and parental law will be recognized as divine law. The person who loves his neighbor as he loves himself will desire the same blessings for others that he himself enjoys. He will not love his neighbor supremely, for that would be idolatry, and he must not love him as he loves himself if his own self-love has reached the stage of idolatry. The demands of the second table of the decalogue presuppose obedience to the first, which makes creature worship impossible.

The decalogue and its demands of love are summed up in the golden rule, *"Therefore all things whatsoever ye would that men should do to you, do ye even so to them: for this is the law and the prophets."* Matthew 7:1:2. The golden rule is declared to be *"the law and the prophets."* It is the law and the Scriptures in daily practice. *"For this is the law and the prophets summed up,"* reads the Weymouth translation, and *"that is the meaning of the law and the*

151

prophets," is the rendering by **James Moffatt.**

The golden rule has been called *"all the Scriptures in a nutshell,"* and the *"incomparable summary."* It is the distilled essence of the decalogue as interpreted by Christian conduct. It is love *"without dissimulation"* or *"hypocrisy"* or without the mask of the actor. In his book, *The Ten Commandments for Today,* page 149, J. B. **Rounds** says: *"No man ever lived the golden rule who did not obey the ten commandments. You cannot really hate the ten commandments and love the golden rule. There cannot be a single one of them broken that does not affect it."*

The thirteenth chapter of *First Corinthians* is a beautiful picture of the law of God when fulfilled by love. It has been appropriately called "The Magna Charta of Love." *"If I can speak with the tongues of men and angels, but am destitute of love, I have but become a loud-sounding trumpet or a clanging cymbal. If I possess the gift of prophecy and am versed in all mysteries and all knowledge, and have such absolute faith that I can remove mountains, but am destitute of love, I am nothing. And if I distribute all my possessions to the poor, and give up my body to be burned, but am destitute of love, it profits me nothing.*

"Love is patient and kind. Love knows neither envy nor jealousy. Love is not forward and self-assertive, nor boastful and conceited. She does not behave unbecomingly, nor seek to aggrandize herself, nor blaze out in passionate anger, nor brood over wrongs. She finds no pleasure in injustice done to others, but joyfully sides with the truth. She knows how to be silent. She is full of trust, full of hope, full of patient endurance. Love never fails."

"And so there remain faith, hope, love-these three; and of these the greatest is love." 1 Corinthians 13:4-8, 13, Weymouth translation.

Surely we must all agree that the greatest need of the church today is love—obedience to that great rule of life and conduct which sums up all that is worth while. How quickly it would banish strife and greed and crime, and bring peace to this war-weary world. To this generation of distress and perplexity, of haunting fears and failing hearts, the Prince of Peace cries out, *"O that thou hadst hearkened to My commandments! then had thy peace been as a river, and thy righteousness as the waves of the sea."* Isaiah 48:18. God grant that it may be writ large in the thinking of modern man that *"God is love,"* and that *"love is the fulfilling of the law."*